INDE

PREFACE

Henry David Thoreau famously said, "Things don't change, people do." If things are to happen, you must make them happen. Good people and businesses always make things happen. Let's look at the essential rules of making things happen.

Rule 1 – Always have a CEO attitude – You must start by taking responsibility for all things both good and bad. Accept that your company signs your check and you fill in the numbers. Your own personal philosophy, which is determined strictly by choice and your own free will, determines your first step in success or failure. We want to introduce or re-introduce you, to the automobile sales division industry.

Rule 2 – Every business operates two businesses: People and Marketing – If you are great with people but don't have people to speak to, you fail. Marketing and Self-Marketing has become essential to all sales people.

Rule 3 – Lead generation equals dollar creation – The more leads you generate the more money you earn. How do you create leads? Develop a marketing plan. Draw a small circle on a piece of paper and put the name of your company in the middle. (Remember: **your** company, not the one that signs your check.) Now draw lines in different directions that look like spokes coming out of the circle. Label each spoke as a source of leads. (Example: walk-ins, incoming sales calls, referrals, repeats, be-backs, service, networking, prospecting etc.) Notice that each spoke can have multiple spokes that sprout from it.

Rule 4 – Build value first – The perception of price is always in relation to the value perceived. Dynamic Presentation greatly increases your chances of making the sale. What do customers perceive to be the value in your offer, product, the business, or you? To create value, you must TLC: think like a customer, and then take action.

Rule 5 – Give HFG - Hope for Gain. People always want something better than what they have; it's human nature. Hope for Gain follows the pleasure versus pain principle of life. People act to either find pleasure or avoid pain. Hope for Gain moves people toward pleasure.

Rule 6 – Offer risk reversal - Take away your customers' risk, and it will create a sense of urgency in the eyes of the customer. You must lower the barriers of entry that discourage customer traffic. Risk reversal allows your customer to avoid pain.

Rule 7 – Provide leverage – Hope for Gain and risk reversal provide leverage for people to act. You must always be thinking of ways that your customers can get excited about contacting you now. Urgency, emotions, social proof, incentives, and testimonials all provide that much needed leverage.

Rule 8 – Facts tell; stories sell- Stories add the most important element of sales and marketing. People think in pictures. People relate to stories in which they can envision themselves in the starring role, so make them the star. People will avoid advertising and marketing on purpose, but they will react to a good story.

Rule 9 – Utilize the law of obligation and reciprocation – In sales or marketing, you must be willing to add the wow factor. You must be willing to give people extra service, extra offers, extra emotion, extra humor, extra enthusiasm... extra everything, until the customer feels an overwhelming obligation to give you a chance.

Rule 10 – Social media is the new way of advertising – If you're looking to improve your situation, regardless of whether you're working for somebody or you own your own business in sales, social media is the only platform that you need to worry about in this market. Facebook and Instagram will become the two most important things that you do. I'm going to elaborate on social media in the later pages of this book, so feel free to jump ahead. The last pages of this book will feature an entire section dedicated to social media as it is one of the most important aspects of the industry in this day and age.

Now let me give you some examples of how to create leads using these rules.

1. Nice trade call – Every time you take a nice trade-in, call at least 20 of your sold customers and let them in on a secret. Let them know about the beautiful vehicle you now have, and how it hasn't been put all the way though service and clean-up yet. Let them know you're calling a few of your preferred customers about the newly acquired vehicle. If they don't want it, ask them who might.

2. Create affiliations – With whom do you want to do business and associate your business with? Always think of how you can add value to them first. What can you do to help their business? Offer coupon swaps or offer to create a coupon for a two-for-one special at their restaurant. In return, ask that they distribute a coupon from your business (Referral Program). In addition to this, talk about creating and maintaining a business partnership with them.

3. Offer a free program – Offer a thirty-minute program to some of the varying associations on how to buy a vehicle. Take brochures with coupons offering a value that would make them

act quickly to receive something of value from you. Create a lead first.

4. Postcards – Postcards are cheap. You can send these to targeted markets with a targeted message, such as, "Employee Purchase Program – Buy a vehicle for what I would pay!"

5. Val-Packs – Postcard advertising made even cheaper.

6. Orphan Owners - Call every orphan owner, (customers not being followed up anymore) and offer them something of value. If you offer all the clients who've not been contacted the chance to do business with you, a large percentage will consider doing more business with you in the future.

7. FSBO call – Call everyone selling their vehicle, and ask them about their trade. Offer to get them a FREE trade appraisal and to help them sell/purchase their vehicle.

8. Create a Free Special Report – "How to buy a vehicle" – You could combine your postcards with this message and once you've created a lead through their response by phone or email, you can follow up after sending your special report. (Did the information help?) This will help to build relationships.

9. Create your own web site – Put your web site address on all your business cards, mailing, materials etc. Put your picture, biography, special offers, free credit report, trade appraisal, etc. Make people go to your site for a special offer.

Don't let what you can't do interfere with what you can do. You can't change economies, but you can work every day to change your actions. A little extra effort put forth everyday will help build a success story. "WHEN THE TIME TO DELIVER HAS COME, THE TIME TO PREPARE HAS GONE"

Make it happen!

I've made an entire living just off craigslist. So, in short, SEO the heck out of your website, and advertise on craigslist. These two sources will give you plenty of business. If you can afford it, dump whatever money you have into Google, Yahoo and Bing, and watch the dollars roll in. Now, in the next sections, you're going to learn what's called the road to sale. This is something that's been in the car business for over 60 years. If you stick to these 12 principles without deviation, you will close deals and make plenty of money.

Now, the following 12 steps or principles can be used if you're just starting in the business with little experience. Let's say you want to spend a year working at a car dealership to gain some sales experience before you dive in and open your own business. These following principles are pretty much laid in stone, so just use these 12 steps no matter what you do. Whether you stay working in a new car store franchise, or you open your own dealership, get ready to enjoy some serious financial freedom.

In these following pages I'm going to break these steps down for you. I'll also give you some phone skills that will definitely be of use to you. The phone scripts that you're going to read over are to be used exactly as they are written as a canned response. You must practice saying naturally just as you would if you were an actor studying lines for a movie.

Road to a Sale Step 1

THE INTRODUCTION

On the Road to a Sale Step 1 appears to be the simplest. All you must do is say, "Hello", right? Successful salespeople know the importance of using a proper meet and greet.

You never get a second chance to make a first impression and psychologists tell us during the first 54 seconds after meeting someone is when it's formed...

If it isn't the correct one, the damage may already be done.

I cringe when I see something that should be so easy become mangled because it is poorly taught or not taught at all.

In many dealerships car sales people begin by approaching the customer with an opening such as...

"Hi, what can we sell you today?" or "Are you here about our big sale?".

What you are about to learn may revolutionize automobile sales as we know it. All you have to say is...

"Welcome to ABC Dealership, may I help you find someone?"...

I told you the Road To a Sale Step 1 should be simple, didn't I?

There are only a handful of responses they might have. Whatever it is, now is your chance to make a lasting impression.

Meet and greets are very important. A firm handshake, looking somebody straight in the eye and introducing yourself are essential to making a good lasting impression. It can be easy to make a negative first impression, so here are some things you want to avoid. Don't wear sunglasses, don't smoke a cigarette, don't eat, or do anything else that would be disrespectful, distracting, or just plain stupid when you're meeting a customer for the first time.

Make sure you are dressed clean and neat. If you plan on wearing shorts and a golf shirt, make sure they're pressed and look professional. Typically, this attire would only be worn if you're an independent dealer, not if you're working at a franchise store. At this point in your career, you should have made yourself some business cards. These cards will look professional and will include your name, phone number, website address, and email address. This is to ensure that customers have a way of contacting you for any future inquiries. I have one additional tip for introductions. If you're talking to a couple, let's say a man and a woman, make sure you shake the hand and address the woman first. Don't assume at any point that the woman or the wife is not the decision-maker of some sort. These kinds of assumptions could be the grave mistake that costs you a customer sale.

Road to a Sale Step 2
FACT FINDING

On the Road to a Sale Step 2 is fact finding. Perform this step correctly, and you will be on the path to making a sale.

What information would be helpful to make certain you are showing the right vehicle to your customer? Would you like to know what terms of sale are important? Wouldn't you like to have an easier close? The road to a sale step 2 is designed to provide these answers.

What are the important things to know? You can build quite a list but here are the ones you must have before you proceed.

- **What will the vehicle be used for?**
  This question will help you select a vehicle to fulfill the customer's need. Towing, taking the family on trips, commuting long distances to work are all examples of needs that buyers consider when purchasing a vehicle.

- **Who is the primary driver?**
  This person has a great influence on the buying decision. Pay attention to what they express as areas of need and want.

- **How many members are in your family?**
  No sense showing a two-seater to a customer who has told you this vehicle is for taking vacations with their five children.

- **What do you like or dislike about your current vehicle?**

Listen carefully. What you will hear are the features that are important to them and which features you should avoid.

▢ **How many miles a year do you typically drive?**
This answer may lead you, at the proper time, to presenting a lease or other type of residual based finance program to your customer.

▢ **What are your current monthly payments?**
It's much easier to ask for only two or three dollars a day more rather than sixty dollars more than they are currently paying, isn't it?

▢ **What do you folks like to do in your spare time?**
Establishing common ground with folks about a hobby or some other activity is a great icebreaker and allows you to become just like them.

▢ **How long have you owned your vehicle?**
The answer may provide a clue about their trade cycle or perhaps some indication of what they may owe on a possible trade in.

Take time to build a list of questions that help you know what your customer is about and what is important to them. By using the Road to a Sale Step 2 to your advantage, you will make more sales and gross profit.

Road to a Sale Step 3

THE SELECTION

On your Road to a Sale Step 3 calls for you to select a vehicle from your current inventory. You will do so based on the information you gathered in Step 2.

Putting your customer on the wrong vehicle is a recipe for disaster. You will struggle when it comes time to ask for the business because there is no urgency to fill a want or need. If you do, make the sale chances are good you will leave gross profit on the table.

At the beginning of the page, it stated the Road to a Sale Step 3 calls for you to select a vehicle from your current inventory. First, we will deal with new vehicles. Why is this important? There are several reasons.

☐ **People get excited about what they can see, feel and touch.**

Showing customers a vehicle as opposed to a brochure helps them take mental ownership. Most dealerships maintain adequate inventory levels to insure there is one that will fit the bill

☐ **You know the history of the vehicle**

Dealer trades are an inevitable part of the car business. In some instances, such as times when inventories are low, they cannot be avoided.

There are additional costs incurred in doing dealer trades. The cost comes from somewhere and that is usually the gross profit. If you have to dealer trade for a vehicle the dealership it is coming from may not take the same care in maintaining their inventory and vehicle condition could present an obstacle.

Many customers object to the mileage being put on their new car. Trailering the vehicle is even more costly. The dealer you are getting the vehicle from may not disclose to your inventory manager additional equipment added at their dealership until after you have made your deal. The customer has a deal, the cost of the extra equipment comes out of your gross profit.

In conclusion, think of a dealer trade like a forward pass in football. Only 3 things can happen, and 2 of them are bad. It's better to make a small price concession for one in stock than risk the hazards of dealer trading.

▢ You have no control over a customer who has left your dealership

If you dealer trade for a vehicle there is nothing preventing your customer from continuing to shop. Think of how many dealerships they will pass on the way home. What if something on the lot catches their eye. They stop, look at it and if they buy it your deal is done. No delivery, no car deal. No car deal, no paycheck.

▢ Broken or missing equipment will kill your deal

When you do not sell out of stock this is the risk you take. You can reassure the customer all you want you will repair what is broken or add what is missing. All you are doing, should they agree, is setting yourself up for a poor customer survey and lowered gross.

⬚ **Taking a vehicle order instead of selling out of stock**

This is another part of the car business that at times is unavoidable. This carries the same risks as dealer trading about not taking your customer out of the buying market. In addition, the wait time often leads your customers to continue shopping. If you must take an order as opposed to selling from stock, have your manager help you tighten up the details to prevent this from happening.

Now most of the steps just mentioned are for those working at a new car franchise. However, let's just say you are an independent dealer. You can go on to your local auctions website or even eBay and look for additional inventory. This is inventory that you can possibly buy for potential customer and use somebody else's inventory for your own stock.

There are some very good websites out there like Manheim.com, Adesa.com, IAAI.com, but you want to stay away from some other independent junk auctions because they let other dealers in there that actually shouldn't be in the business. If you just use some of these main ones you find yourself in a better position to make smart buying decisions.

eBay has always been a very good source. For example, in their eBay motors section, you can find a wide range of vehicles from classic muscle cars to a brand-new Shelby Mustang. I personally found some very good deals on their own cars that I bought and was able to flip. eBay does have their share of cons. They are a little bit expensive; I believe their listing fees run around $54, which is on the pricier side. In addition, they do not have the best customer support when it comes to people not paying for a bid that they won. It's important to know about these drawbacks just in case you want to use eBay's selling store as an additional source for listing your vehicles online. Even though eBay is a very good source, they have poor follow-up and don't screen the people bidding well enough to make sure that they had the means to pay for those auctions. Finally, whatever you do, the last thing you want to do is sign up for PayPal. This is just my opinion, but in my experience, it will be absolutely no help to you at all. If anything, all PayPal does is keep your money for long periods of time and will tie up your cash.

The best thing you can do is get yourself signed up with a local credit card company set up a payment option on your website. Then, direct people from eBay to your website and make your purchase that way. even Although I am a big promoter of eBay and eBay motors, trust me when I tell you set up your payment option a different way. This is a great source to buy and sell inventory nationally.

If you choose to use eBay, go through their eBay University motors. It will definitely prove to be an excellent educational experience for you, and it will give you some very good advice as well as help you with some technical knowledge.

Road to a Sale Step 4

THE WALK AROUND

In the Road to a Sale Step 4, your customer finds themselves owning and using the vehicle. As you present the vehicle remember to use a feature-function-benefit sales presentation. It is here if you need to review. Your product presentation will include the features you determined during Step 2, Fact Finding, that are important to your customer. **Where you start your presentation has a great bearing on moving to the demonstration drive.**

Begin your presentation at the front of the vehicle. Highlight styling, impact resistant bumpers, lexan headlamp covers, etc.

Then lift the hood and present the components contained in the engine compartment. Give emphasis to customer hot buttons. Ease of owner use while checking fluid levels, a mention of horsepower and torque if appropriate, anything that is special about the engine itself such as variable valve timing, etc. When you have completed your engine compartment presentation you will...

Move to the driver side of the vehicle at the front fender. This is the time to highlight, still using good feature-function-benefit presentation methods, tires, braking systems, upgraded wheels, etc. This is also a good time to point out paint finish and protection. When you have concluded this part of the Road to a Sale Step 4, you will...

Move to the driver door and open it. This is the time to show, if so equipped, the power driver seat and its functions. Do not make the mistake of waiting until you are in the vehicle. It is much easier to operate from a standing position outside the car. Just another reminder to your customer of how easy this vehicle is to operate, right? Mention the interior fabric, leather, etc. Show them how much room is provided for ease of entry and exit. **DO NOT GET IN THE VEHICLE OR HAVE YOUR CUSTOMER DO SO.**

When you are finished move to the rear.

Here is where you can show the trunk capacity, any special features such as trailer equipment, anti-slip rear axles, etc. Styling is good to re-emphasize as well. If you are showing a truck during the Road to a Sale Step 4, use this time to show the functionality of the bed, two-tier loading, removable tailgate and any other feature that builds value. Upon completing your presentation at the rear of the vehicle, you will...

Move to the rear passenger door.
Here is where, in almost all cases you will find the Monroney Label. This is the window sticker on the vehicle. Point out standard features and all optional equipment. Fuel economy, on vehicles under 8600 GVW, are also listed here. Open the rear door and demonstrate how the child safety locks operate. If the vehicle has a built-in entertainment center, this is the time to show it. When you are satisfied you have left nothing out, it is time to

Move to the front passenger door and open it.
Before you ask your customer to get in show the power seat from outside the vehicle. Give your customer a bird's eye view of the interior styling. Show any other special equipment. Now it is time to **tell your customer to sit in the vehicle.**

I told you at the beginning of the Road to a Sale Step 4 where you start your presentation has a great bearing on transitioning to the demo drive.

Help the other family members in, and then go to the driver door and get in.

Don't forget the weather. Start the vehicle and make certain you adjust the temperature to one that is comfortable. You are going to use some time showing the operating controls. Show your customer how easy they are to use. Highlight the readability of the instrument panel. Ask them their favorite radio station and use it while demonstrating the stereo system. Point out leg, hip and headroom. Do not forget to use solid feature-function-benefit while doing so.

When you have finished your interior presentation it is time to

Take a demonstration drive.
Always use the same route, make certain your management team knows you are away from the lot, and make right hand turns only. Select a route that allows your customer to experience several types of driving conditions. These could be highways, surface streets and neighborhoods.

Always drive first. Why? Because your customer is still not comfortable with the operating controls. The time you spend driving will allow them to become comfortable and more importantly, if you are speaking to them if they drive first they will not pay attention to you...they are concentrating on where the controls are, avoiding an accident, etc.

When you return to the dealership tell your customer to park in front of the building. DO NOT LET THEM park the vehicle in the space it came out of. You will find that in almost all instances your customer will, when parked, immediately turn off the vehicle. This is the time for you to ask **the single most important question in the car business...**

"Other than the numbers, is there anything preventing us from doing business today?"

Before you continue on the Road to a Sale Step 4, find out if you have left any unanswered objections or neglected to show something of importance. If you have, it will come up during your negotiations. It is better to answer them now.

Here are things you should think about prior to the Road to a Sale Step 4.

▢ **Is the vehicle ready to show?**
If your customer is an appointment, take time well before their expected arrival and check the condition of the vehicle. Is it clean? Does it have fuel? Are there any warning lights that need to be addressed?

▢ **Are you ready?**
Is your product knowledge where it should be? Can you comfortably use feature-function-benefit to present the vehicle? Have you done a good job of fact finding?

The importance of product presentation If you have addressed these issues and are confident, your customer will feel your professionalism and confidence.

Road to a Sale Step 5

THE TRADE IN

The Road to a Sale Step 5 is about evaluating a customer's trade-in. Before we go any further make certain you understand that **evaluating the trade-in is not placing a value on it.** That responsibility is left for a member of management.

We are going to deal with evaluating as it relates to physical and mechanical condition. Do a good job here, and you can assure your customer the allowance they receive for their trade is a good one based on market conditions and comparison.

Your customer has, in spite of what they may say, a preconceived idea as to what they think their vehicle is worth. There is some information here that will show how some of your customers find that figure.

During the Road to a Sale Step 5 you have certain things you need to do. Here is a list to help you get started on making sure you do this correctly.

- **Fill out the appraisal slip accurately**
  There is a reason your dealership uses a particular form. Accurate and complete information will make the process quicker and smoother. Pay particular attention to year model and mileage. Do not take your customer's word for what year model their vehicle is. Some people, believe it or not, do not know. Look at the vehicle identification number. The 8th digit from the right will tell you. Familiarize yourself with reading year model codes from the VIN.

☐ **Do not leave your customer for any longer than is necessary**

Many salespeople make the mistake of taking the trade-in to be appraised and waiting for the manager to complete his appraisal. This is a mistake. There may be several vehicles awaiting an appraisal. You may arrive at your used car department and find the manager is out appraising another vehicle. Take the appraisal slip and keys to a manager and return to your customer as quickly as possible. Why?
Because the more time you spend away from your customer the more you allow them to question whether they are "done shopping", wonder if "they are doing the right thing", etc.

☐ **Have your customer help you with the information you need**

Again, remind yourself to spend the least amount of time away from your customer. Have them help you by getting the mileage for you. Why? Because when they read the mileage as 72,837 miles it will remind them that it's not 70,000 miles and also reinforce the principle that mileage plays a large part in valuing a trade.

Have the customer walk around their trade-in with you. If you will touch a dent or scratch, they will tell you what happened. Physical condition is a part of value. Ask them what major mechanical repair was last done or suggested.

Here is a simple statement that will help you get your customer involved in the trade evaluation...

"Mr. Customer, I want to present your trade-in to my used car buyer in the best possible light. Would you mind trading places with me for a few moments and sell me your car?"

Your customer will, at some point, ask you what YOU think their vehicle is worth. Do not put yourself in the trick bag. Road to a Sale Step 5 is about evaluation, not value.

YOUR JOB IS NOT TO PLACE A DOLLAR FIGURE ON THE TRADE. DO NOT FALL INTO THIS TRAP. IF YOU GIVE THEM A FIGURE THAT IS TOO HIGH OR TOO LOW YOU HAVE CREATED THE CONDITIONS FOR MISTRUST AND LOSS OF CREDIBILITY

Try this instead...

"Mr. Customer, our used car buyers look at thousands of vehicles each month both here at the dealership and at auctions. They stay current on market values and I know they will have a much better figure in mind than I would. I would hate to cost you money or miss your business by giving you inaccurate information, wouldn't you agree?"

Now, let's just touch on the trade-in a little bit more. Again, most of the steps listed above in this section are for if you're working at a franchise store for somebody else and you're not an independent dealer. So, let's say you are an independent dealer, what you do if somebody has a car, they want to trade you for. Here you go what are your sources Heidi figure out what this car is worth because you are using your own money. The best ways to sign up and get a subscription to NADA.COM. This is the best and the only source I feel that is good to give you an accurate trade-in value regardless of where you're located in this country. And obviously you want to use average trade-in value that the book is going to state, and you can deduct or add for equipment and mileage.

NADA stands for National Automotive Dealers Association. This is the governing body and the main source for the automotive business, but there are other sources out there like Kelly Blue Book, Gallops, Galves, and Auto Trader. All these other sources will never give you a realistic true value on what a vehicle is worth even though some people find them to be good sources my opinion is to stick to NADA. The other thing you can do when you're evaluating a trade is go to Manheim.com. If you're signed up with them, then look at their online tool called MMR. This will give you the very current auction data on what that vehicle will be selling for at the auction. Between these two sources will give you a great idea of what your trade-in is worth and what you should pay for anything really after that is good to be a matter of your own opinion of what you think that cars worth.

Now, one thing you can be sure of is that a car in the Northeast is not worth the same in the southeast. I see them as much is a $1500 difference for the exact same vehicle with the same miles, it just depends on where you're located, in what part of the country. Just try to stick to your guns and follow these two simple rules and you shouldn't get hurt when you're taking in a trade. The other thing is a lot of people like to use Carfax. This is a bloated overrated program that's expensive. In my opinion, you're better off using Autocheck.com, this gives you the same information as Carfax, but is more accurate. Most of the auto auctions use it, and it's a third of the price.

Road to a Sale Step 6

THE PROCESS

Get seated and relaxed. The Road to a Sale Step 6 calls for your customer to do just that. This may seems like something that on the surface is so obvious and easy to accomplish that it might not require much thought. Or does it?

This step is often left to chance because very few salespeople think about it. What is not spelled out in most auto sales training programs is the customer needs to be seated and relaxed **in an atmosphere that makes it easier for your customer to conduct business.**

What atmosphere does your office or workspace present?

- **Free of clutter?**
  Your customers like to do business with professionals. A clean, uncluttered office or desk area will present that image. Do you have worksheets from previous deals spread all over your desk? Do you look organized and ready for business? It takes only a few moments to tidy up, and it pays big dividends.

- **How is your furniture arranged?**
  Do you have adequate seating for everyone? Is it arranged to allow you to move in and out as you go to the desk for numbers?

▢ **Do you have awards and certifications prominently displayed?**
People like to do business with winners and experts. Show your customers you are proud of your achievements.

▢ **Are you able to turn off your telephone?**
If so, make a big gesture of it. It shows the customer you are interested in only them. If not, call the switchboard and tell them to hold your calls, you are with a customer. It will make an impression.

▢ **Are there any hidden distractions?**
The volume on a radio? Any odd odors from something in the trash can? The condition of the floor? Leave nothing to chance.

Before you ask your customers to be seated do everyone, including yourself, a big favor. Chances are you have spent quite some time in Steps 1 to 5. Show your customers where the restroom facilities are. Ask if they would like a soft drink or water.

As your transition from Step 6 to Step 7, a customer who suddenly needs to take a restroom break or get a drink is a momentum killer.

Road to a Sale Step 7

THE CLOSE

It is time to trial close as the Road to a Sale Step 7 calls for. Why is it referred to as a trial close and not just a close? For one very simple reason...**this is where you allow your customer to bring up any objections you may have left unanswered or express anything that might stop them from doing business with you.**

At the conclusion of the demonstration drive you asked them the single most important question...

"Other than the numbers, is there anything stopping us from doing business today?"

At that point, you answer any further objections. Now is the time to find out if anything has been overlooked. You can do that by saying to your customer

"Mr. Customer, we've agreed that other than the numbers there is nothing stopping us from doing business. Here are some of the forms we will be using."

If there are no other objections you are ready to continue with the Road to a Sale Step 7. If there are, it is time to answer them. Now, open your folder with all the forms needed to complete a car deal. What? You don't keep folders with all the documents you will need to do a deal? Shame on you. Professional salespeople should have several sets at the ready, at all times. What documents should you include?

- A buyer's order or deal worksheet

- An appraisal slips

- Customer statement or credit application

- Any other documentation required to complete a car deal

Make certain you have answered any question the customer may have asked before you write anything on a form. Once you have done so take out each form and introduce them to your customer. Do not make the mistake many of your peers make by taking out a worksheet and writing their name on it. Why? Because if you do chances are the customer will say this...

"Hang on a minute, I'm not buying anything." Sound familiar?

Avoid this by taking the forms, one at a time, and showing them to your customer. Here are easy word scripts to use as you do so.

- **The Buyer's order or worksheet**
  "Mr. Customer, on this form I am going to put some information about the vehicle you are purchasing and the vehicle you are trading in." Now lay the form face down.

- **The appraisal slip**
  "Mr. Customer, this is the form we used when we looked at your trade-in. I will take it, along with your vehicle to my used car buyer." Lay the form aside.

- **The customer statement or credit application**
  "This is the form we will use to provide information to our lenders." Put the form aside.

☐ **Any other documents?**
Use the same format to let your customer become familiar with them.

Now, it is time to take the buyer's order or worksheet and write their name on it. Because they have already seen it, they know that it is the form you will use for the information about them and the vehicles being purchased and traded in.

You have now completed the Road to a Sale Step 7 and are ready to move to step 8, the write-up.

Road to a Sale Step 8
THE COMMITMENT

In the Road to a Sale Step 8, you will get a written commitment to do business based on all terms being agreeable. I will assume you have done the first seven steps properly. If you need to review them go here.

The terms that need to be agreeable to your customer are Selling Price, Trade Allowance, Down Payment and Monthly Payment. There is an in-depth discussion of each of these at the following links.

In Step 7, you took a few moments to introduce the customer to the forms you will be using. By doing that when you begin to write on your worksheet you will avoid having the customer say..."**Hold on, I'm not buying anything.**"

As you start your write-up, take a moment to reassure the customer.

"**Mr. Customer, we know most misunderstandings are due to a lack of communication. I am going to write down exactly what our obligation to you is so that we can avoid any chance of that.**"

Now proceed to complete the information your dealership requires before you receive figures from the sales desk.

As you write you may hear additional objections from your customer. **Stop and address them now.** If you do not, they will pop up later, I guarantee it. You may have to go as far as to go out to the vehicle and re-present or re-demo. If that is what is required, take the time to do so. Shortcuts lead to pay cuts.

Before you leave to go to the desk, tell your customers what you are doing. Explain to them you are going to management to get a proposal. Do not leave them wondering where you are.

This is a bit off topic but stop and think about what is happening in the Road to a Sale Step 8. You are asking the customer for a commitment to do business. You will get figures from the desk and you will be forced to leave your customers at your desk/office. In most dealerships the desk is visible from your work area. Your customers are watching you. **Be careful how you act.** You and I cannot change human nature. This is time to be business-like. If your customers see you laughing or joking at the desk, they will assume they are the topic of conversation. It is what it is. Working with the desk is a topic covered here.

After you get your figures from the desk, make certain you understand each of them. If your dealership pencils deals using the 4 square presentation you can find information on that here.

Road to a Sale Step 9

NEGOTIATION

The Road to a Sale Step 9 is about negotiation and closing. In the first 8 steps, you have set the stage for finalizing your deal. **This step is like the game of golf. You practice on the range and test what you have learned on the course.**

It is time to test what occurred in the first 8 steps. If you need to review them go here.

Negotiation with your customer involves the terms of sale. You received them from the sales desk and this step is about presenting them. But before you do there is detailed information about that here.

On this page you need to learn or refresh your knowledge of negotiation. The first rule is...
You can only negotiate one item at a time.

An illustration here is helpful. Suppose you are presenting figures to your customer. Prior to the write-up they asked about an accessory. Let's use floor mats as an example. You present the figures to your customer. The floor mats are priced at $149.00. The customer says..."Wow, I can get floor mats for a lot less than that." This may or may not be true, but do not lose focus on what is important here.

You can either negotiate the price of floor mats or you can negotiate the terms of the sale.

The mistake salespeople make here is becoming involved in a lengthy negotiation about floor mat pricing. They give all sorts of reasons and justifications about why the quoted price for the mats is fair. Yes, the Road to a Sale Step 9 is about negotiation but remember which one is most important. They may win this negotiation, but they have lost focus on the sale of the vehicle. And so, has the customer.

Instead of getting off focus why not say,

"Mr. Customer, I am certain my dealership would not miss your business over just a couple of dollars for floor mats. I will work on that figure for you, but before I do, I want to make certain the rest of the figures are agreeable."

Now you have the customer, and yourself, back on track. You are negotiating the terms of sale. Accessories are certainly a part, but they are not the main focus.

One thing you must remember is don't fall in love with the inventory; sell everything you can regardless of the profit. I promise you can replace any vehicle that you buy with another one. There's an old saying that says there's an ass for every seat, and I promise you that is the truth even if you're making $100 sell it. Or maybe you're losing money, the best customer is the one in front of you waiting to pay you. Don't pass, don't be a fool and sell the car.

Road to a Sale Step 10
FINANCE

Congratulations! It's time to take your customer to finance, and the Road to a Sale Step 10 will show you the right way. Remember, you can return to any step in the road to a sale by clicking here.

Before we continue, I want to make certain you know something about the function of your finance department. Your dealership may refer to it as the "business office" or "F&I" (finance and insurance).

What does the finance department do? It varies slightly from dealership to dealership, but here is a list of their most important duties.

- **Secure your car deal**
  Their primary job is to secure your car deal. They complete all necessary documentation. This includes Lender contracts, title work documents, powers of attorney, etc.

- **They are a profit center for your dealership and your help in making the transition a smooth one is critical.**

  Your finance department offers products to protect your customer's investment. They offer extended service agreements and insurance programs that pay the debt in the event your customer becomes disabled or passes away. They have programs for paint and finish protection and tire replacement.

▣ **They secure financing for your customer**
At most dealerships, the finance department interviews the customer and completes the credit application or customer statement. Based on that information, they present the deal package to the lenders they know will offer your customer not only the best available rate but approve the deal. Because of the volume of business dealerships like yours send to lenders your business office can offer rates the customer may not have access to at their financial institution.

How do people become finance directors or producers? Your finance department is staffed by people who most likely started right where you are. On the sales floor. They demonstrated the ability to close deals and maintain great customer satisfaction scores. Finance department employees are among the best salespeople in your dealership.

Always remember the rules of your dealership take precedence over any training you receive here. Having said that I will share with you a simple turn to the business office.

"Mr. Customer, this is Joe. He is one of our finance directors, and you are in great hands. He does a terrific job for my customers. I am going to get your vehicle ready for delivery. See you in just a few minutes."

Unless your dealership asks you to mention extended service agreements or other products offered by your finance department...

Road to a Sale Step 11

DELIVERY

The Road to a Sale Step 11 is about proper vehicle delivery. As a reminder, you can review any of the previous steps.

In order to insure you make a proper delivery, use the delivery checklist that your dealership has developed or the one automobile manufacturers provide with each new vehicle. Familiarize yourself with the items they include.

Many dealerships have a dedicated delivery coordinator. This individual is charged with the responsibility of delivering the vehicle to the customer. This is to insure your dealership's customer satisfaction ratings remain at or above the standards established by the manufacturer.

If your dealership has such a person, it does not relieve you of the responsibility of knowing what the road to a sale step 11 is all about.

You are required to make follow-up calls to your new owners at prescribed intervals. Knowing what is on the delivery checklist will give you a guideline to follow when making these calls.

If your customer has a concern, address it now and make the necessary arrangements to correct the problem...do not wait.

Making a proper delivery during the Road to a Sale Step 11 and receiving great customer satisfaction scores are a vital part of your job description. Here are the elements that lead to achieving those great scores.

- **Is the vehicle clean and free from defects?**
  This is the number one cause of poor scores. Do not leave anything to chance. After the vehicle leaves the clean-up area inspect it yourself. Act as if you are the buyer. Is it up to the standard you would expect?

- **Is it full of gas?**
  In the rush to deliver the car, this is often overlooked. This is the number 2 cause of poor scores, by the way.

- **How about the radio?** Many dealerships ask the customer to list their favorite radio stations. While the customer is in the finance office, they pre-set the stations for the customer. This is a really nice and memorable touch.

- **What arrangements need to be made for additional equipment?**
  If your customer purchased dealer installed or aftermarket equipment, they will want to know how soon they can get the work performed. While they are in the business office talk to your service department or vendor to schedule the work.

I want to take a side step here. This is important enough to stop and talk about right now. Anything made by human hands is subject to breaking or malfunction. The new vehicle you are delivering may unfortunately experience one of those problems. You and your dealership are anxious to see they are corrected; after all the Road to a Sale Step 11 requires you to cover the manufacturer's warranty, right?

IF YOU HAVE A CUSTOMER WHO IS EXPERIENCING A PROBLEM, STOP AND THINK BEFORE YOU DO ANYTHING ELSE.

I learn better when someone uses an example, so let's use one here. You are paged to the phone. It is a customer who recently bought a vehicle from you. Something isn't working or needs to be repaired, so you assure the customer your dealership will get it taken care of, right? Of course. Here is where the problems start.

Most salespeople say to the customer, "Mr. Customer, no problem. Just bring it in and we'll take care of things."

You have just created the conditions for a potential disaster.

Why? Because now your customer is going to get in their vehicle and come to your dealership. How does that cause a potential disaster? Simple. When they get to your dealership, they will go directly to the service drive.

The service advisors are caught completely off guard. The customer says, "My new car has a problem. The salesperson told me to bring it in." What happens next is common. The service advisor says, "What is the problem?" To which the customer replies, "I told the salesperson. Did he not tell you I was coming?" The advisor says, "No, and as you can see, we have a full schedule of work. It may be a while before we can even look at it." Now the customer is irritated. Not only is no one aware they were coming, now they have an unanticipated wait before anyone even looks at the car.

You can see where this is going, right? The customer comes to the showroom floor to find you.

I will stop here, it doesn't get any better. The Road to a Sale Step 11 is about proper delivery. It is also about proper customer service.

How to avoid the problem? It's easy if you will think before you act.

Let's go back to when you got the phone call. Instead of telling them to "just bring it in", do this instead.

1. **Tell them you are sorry they are having a problem.**
2. **Assure them they will be taken care of.**
3. **Ask them when would be convenient for them to come to the dealership.**
4. **Tell them you will go directly to the service department and inform them of the problem.**
5. **Ask them what number you can call them back at.**
6. **Tell them to give you a few moments.**
7. **Go to the service department and tell a service advisor.**
8. **Call the customer back from the service drive.**
9. **Tell them you are with the advisor who will be taking care of them.**
10. **Hand the phone to the advisor.**

Your dealership pays service advisors to take care of customers, so let them do their job. It creates an opportunity for a better customer experience.

A proper job in the Road to a Sale Step 11 will make your life easier when the time comes to follow up after the sale and ask for referrals.

Let me give you a piece of advice for if you're an independent dealer and something is wrong with the vehicle that you sold. Either fix it or take the car back get it fixed and sell to somebody else. Your potential loss of business and income will far exceed anything that you can possibly imagine if you stick somebody with a bad car; it's not worth it ever. If you are working at a franchise store, dabble full-blown service department to take care of any problems or issues that your customers going to have.

If you're an independent dealer and you're selling your vehicles online, don't forget about Google Plus, Yelp, Facebook, and Twitter. Trust me when I tell you the list is endless of bad reviews you will get by selling one bad car. You can possibly destroy the future of your business by just having a problem. Be an honest dealer and put yourself in the customer shoes. If something goes wrong with that car in the first 30 days, hopefully you've made enough money that you can stand behind it and not blow the customer off. This would be the wrong thing to do in every way shape and form.

If a customer calls you and has a problem with the vehicle you sold them, whether you're working for franchise or working for yourself, the first words that come out in your mouth should be,

"Not a problem, I'm sorry you're having an issue but I will definitely take care of that for you and get your issue resolved." This will put your customer at ease immediately, and you guys will be able to have an intelligent conversation. The customer is not always right. By defusing the situation immediately and not having a confrontation with them, you will put this customer at ease discuss the issue and hopefully rectify it.

The only thing that'll happen after that is you will get positive reviews from that same customer, and it's okay for you to ask for because you took care of their issue anytime within that 30-day period. And it's up to you if you want to extend it further than that, but this way the customer that bought the vehicle from you should have full confidence in who they bought it from and spread that word. That word-of-mouth is worth everything.

Road to a Sale Step 12
REFERRALS-FOLLOW UP

It's over. Or is it? The Road to a Sale Step 12 will teach you that making the sale is only the beginning...or it should be. Most sales training programs identify this step as "Ask for referrals and follow-up." What they recommend is correct, but the order is wrong.

Following up and then asking for referrals is the proper order, and in the Road to a Sale step 12 module you will find out why. I have seen many training articles and methods that teach there is no better time to ask for a referral than at the time of the sale. I disagree. Immediately asking for a referral gives your customer the impression you are done with them and on to the next one.

When is the best time to ask for referrals? The best time is each time you choose to contact your customers. That being said, let's talk about the time table for proper follow-up.

Here is a list of when and some recommendations for the content of your contact.

☐ **Within 24 hours after delivery**
This should be a personal phone call. First, to thank them for their business and the confidence and trust they placed in you and your dealership. Second, to make sure there are no issues that need to be resolved. Perhaps something is not working properly on the vehicle. Before you tell them to "just bring it"

and create the potential for a disaster re-read Step 11 and avoid this common mistake.

[?] **3 Days after delivery**
Your customer has now had a chance to show their vehicle to their friends, family and co-workers. This is the perfect time to ask for referrals. When one person in a particular group gets a new vehicle, it starts a chain reaction. Now everyone begins to think about a new vehicle.

[?] **10 days after delivery**
This contact is to once again make certain your customer is not experiencing any problems. They are about 10-12 days away from receiving the manufacturer's survey. Take this opportunity to address any issues that would lead to a poor score.

[?] **30 days after delivery**
This contact does a couple of things. One, it shows the customer you are there for service after the sale. Two, it once again allows you to ask for a referral. Remind your customer to send in a completely satisfied survey if they have not done so already.

The time table presented in the Road to a Sale Step 12 is only a guide. Your dealership may have a different set of dates and if so, use those. The content and purpose of the contact is what is important.

So... how do you ask for referrals?

You could pick up the phone and say, "Hi Mr. Customer. This is Joe from ABC Dealership. You don't know anyone looking for a car, do you?" Or you could dress it up and say something flowery like, "Hi Mr.

Customer, this is Joe from ABC Dealership. I want to provide the same great deal and service to your friends..." blah, blah, blah.

Do you really think that 10 seconds before your call your customer was thinking, "Boy, I wish ol' Joe would call. I am dying to give him the name of someone who needs a car."

That would be nice, but this is the real world. Just as every call should have a purpose, so should a call be asking for referral business. What purpose is that? To get referrals you say? Yes.

But "how" is the trick. I hope you agree with me that neither of the two methods in the previous paragraph are really very effective.

How about approaching it from another angle? **Instead of calling to ask them for something how about a call to give them some information?** Here is a much better approach for getting referrals during the road to a sale step 12.

"Mr. Customer, this is Joe from ABC Dealership. Did I catch you at a convenient moment? Good, the reason for my call is simple. I know you are not in the market for a vehicle since you just bought a new one, but we just traded for a nice little '02 Toyota Corolla that would make a terrific second car for someone. You don't know anyone looking for a car for a student or just something to commute in, do you?"

Now, remember what I said earlier. When people get a new vehicle, they want to show it off to everyone. The "new car fever" sets in. It's on everyone's mind. So, your customer might just say..."You know, Joe. The other day at work Bill was talking about buying his daughter a car for college." Now, how easy is it to ask for Bill's contact info from your customer and ask if they would mind if you told Bill they suggested you call?

Repeat and referral business is your lifeblood. Use the Road to a Sale Step 12 effectively and build your business.

One thing I want to mention about referrals is get your customers to post online reviews about you on Google Plus, Facebook, Twitter, Yelp, or any other website source that you're using. The more reviews you get, especially if you're an independent dealer, the better off your business is going to flourish. In this day and age, people use the Internet for I imagine just about everything. When it's coming to buying a vehicle, they definitely look online look at cars first. They then look up the dealer rating and see how positive it is. I have many times seen these reviews make or break car deals. Make sure when you're selling a car to a customer, and they are one hundred percent satisfied, that they leave a review for you. Hopefully, they will do it before they leave your office, but if not, you want to do everything in your power to get them to leave that review.

This will be one of the best goals you will have because if you get enough reviews and of course the positive ones you can promote that in many different ways. Especially if you're an independent dealer, these reviews could be your lifeblood. If you're salesperson at a franchise store this also can be extremely important to the future of your independent business inside of that franchise.

COMMON SENSE PREVENTS
COMMON ERRORS

We all make mistakes. Learn from your mistakes and prevent these simple errors.

TAKING SHORTCUTS

Shortcuts lead to pay cuts! The Road to the Sale was designed as a set of building blocks that make it easy. Use them to your advantage.

NOT MAINTAINING A POSITIVE ATTITUDE

Whether you think you can or think you can't...you are right. How important is this? High performers are positive people.

NOT LISTENING TO THE CUSTOMER

When you are talking, the only thing you will hear is something you already know. Listen to the customer. They will tell you exactly what to do, or not to do, to earn their business.

POOR FACT FINDING

You must have information and Step 2 will show you how.

NOT SELLING YOUR ORGANIZATION

There are many benefits to doing business with your company. Tell people what they are.

A POOR PRESENTATION

If you are not enthusiastic how can you expect anyone else to be? Learn how to give a **World Class Presentation** in Step 4.

NOT ANSWERING QUESTIONS

Your customer didn't ask just to hear themselves talk. Unanswered questions become suspicions in the mind of your customer. These questions become hot buttons. Answer them by using this.

NOT FOLLOWING UP

Stay in regular contact with your customers. Do you have an effective follow up system? Send e-mails, letters, postcards. A personalized newsletter really makes an impact.

LOSING CREDIBILITY

A FATAL ERROR
Incorrect information, inattentional misinformation, lack of product knowledge and poor attitude will cost you deals. Walk, talk and act like a professional at all times.

APPEARING ARGUMENTATIVE

Errors like this are hard to overcome. **You will win the battle and lose the war.** Keep control of your emotions. Present logical reasons why and justify your position, but never argue.

Now, here are a lot of different common selling errors that you can look at. Poor fact-finding, taking shortcuts, and not listening to your customer are some of the biggest problems be smart listen to what this person is telling you that's trying to buy a car from you whether your franchise or you're an independent dealer. You know selling your reputation and your business is so important even if you're just a small business,but if you're getting all these positive reviews online you get to use that to your advantage and show people reasons why you should be buying from me and not from buying some somebody else.

If you do a poor presentation on the car that you're selling by not knowing what you're selling, or you have poor product knowledge, I'm sorry but that's just plain stupid. You have to know more than the customer, you have to be the expert, and you have to be the go-to guy when it comes to the car that that customer is buying. If you're an independent dealer go to Wikipedia, Edmonds, Kelly blue book, there is also a whole bunch of sources out there including the manufacturer's website that can give you information on the used or new car that you're selling.

Learn the warranty information, the maintenance information, the features, and benefits of the vehicle that you're trying to sell. Whether you're a franchise or an independent it just doesn't matter; you need to be the product knowledge expert. The other thing is not following up after you sold somebody a car. You just took somebody's money, usually it's a lot of it, so make them feel like you care. You should care because people don't just buy one car, they buy tons of cars. Friends, family relatives, all these people could be your potential future prospects and customers if you do business the right way.

Always, and I mean always, have a positive attitude. No matter what the situation or how rude somebody is, keep your composure and have a positive attitude. Nobody wakes up in the morning planning on having a bad day. But, when that bad day comes, you're going to have to rise above the occasion and have a positive attitude whether you like it or not. Don't get mad at your money because that's all you be doing by having a bad attitude.

Don't take shortcuts. Try to stick to the Steps 1 through 12. Sometimes, customers will try to lead you down a path that you don't want to go, try not to buy into it. Stick with Steps 1 through 12, have a positive attitude, proper fact-finding skills and an ear for good listening and it should be a breeze.

The Common Traits of Winners

Everyone wants to know the formula for success. What common traits are shared by people at the top? There are countless books, studies, charts, and graphs that purport to give us the answers. As you well know there is only one number one in any organization. You can be that person if you have knowledge drive by desire and motivation. Let's look at what winners do.

They Know What is at Stake

Having a winning attitude means you know what you have at risk. Your paycheck, your reputation and the welfare of you and your family. Part of that attitude is knowing that nothing is perfect. You are not perfect; your dealership and management team are not and sometimes the systems and processes in place aren't. Sometimes we fail. Develop an attitude about winning like this sport HALL OF FAMER

Winners Play for Keeps

Life is not a dress rehearsal. You are doing what **you** have chosen to do. Do not accept common. Make the most of it. Do your best always. Never think of your job as something you are doing until something better comes along.

They Strive for Excellence

Winners strive for excellence at everything they do. Do not accept anything less than YOUR personal best in every area of your life.

They Never Stop Learning

Driven people want to know everything about their chosen profession. They read constantly. They know that self-improvement means bigger paydays. They ask those with a record of success for tips and encouragement.

They Never Give Up

They do not consider failure an option. **It just never occurs to them.** They find a way to win. They overcome obstacles. They know it's going to happen, it's only a matter of time. Babe Ruth is most likely the most famous of all baseball players and for many decades held the record for most home runs in a career. What few realize is for decades he held the record for most strikeouts as well. We all, from time to time, come up short of the goal. Never giving up and continuing to reach for the prize is a winner's attitude.

They Practice Self Discipline

I am not sure this should be called a common trait. Self-discipline is so uncommon. How many times have we heard, "I need to lose weight...I think tomorrow I will start to eat less", yet tomorrow never seems to come. Same thing with exercise, overcoming bad habits, prospecting, self-improvement...the list is seemingly endless. Winners know that yesterday is gone, tomorrow is not here and today is the day. They have a game plan, do you? What is your daily plan?

IN ORDER TO RISE ABOVE THE COMPETITION, YOU MUST BE WILLING TO DO WHAT THEY

ARE EITHER UNABLE OR UNWILLING TO DO.

Believe in yourself! Have faith in your abilities! Without a humble but reasonable confidence in your own powers, you cannot be successful or happy.

Always be yourself, express yourself, have faith in yourself, do not go out and look for a successful personality and duplicate it.

The difference between a successful person and others is not a lack of strength or knowledge, but rather a lack of will.

The attempt to combine wisdom and power has only rarely been successful, and then only for a short while.

One of the things you can do is to make yourself a daily game plan. This is probably one of the most important things you can do is plan for tomorrow. Don't just sit there on your butt watching TV or searching the Internet picking your nose. Make your day successful if you have the ability to plan out the entire week or month. Set your game plan, put in the play, and make it work. Nothing is going to fall in your lap; you have to work hard work long hours and put in all the effort in order to reap any of the benefits.

Always plan out the next day. Know what you're going to do, how you're going to do it, and don't give up until your goal for that days hit whether it's selling the car or getting other things in your house in order so that you can make sure that money is made that day. The most un-successful people I know don't have a game plan for what they're going to do. How many professional sports teams do you know go out and take the field without a game plan, I'm going to tell you, it's none. No matter what, the other team, does, they have their game plan and are going to stick to it and executed. Guess what, my friend? You're absolutely no different.

DAILY ACTIVITY FOR SUCCESS

People develop a daily series of routine steps. Have you noticed if the steps get out of order something doesn't seem quite right? If you brush your teeth before you shower notice how showering and then brushing your teeth makes you stop and think about the rest of your routine. Your sales day is the same way. Develop a routine and stick with it. Be prepared. In fifteen minutes, you can prepare for sales success.

Professional salespeople know where they are headed.

What to do First

You have a customer base that needs your attention.

- The ones who did not buy.
- People that did buy
- Previous sold customers that need attention.

Let's take them one at a time

The ones who did not buy. Give priority to this set of people. They need to receive follow up from you by telephone. Before you pick up the phone **your call must have a purpose.**

Think about what you want to say. Calling and saying, "Hi, Mr. Buyer, this is me and I just want to see if you are still in the market," is a waste of his time and yours.
Give your customer a reason for calling.
"Hi, Mr. Jones. This is Bill Smith from ABC Company and after I spoke with you yesterday, I realized I forgot to mention...." Now you are providing something of value. You do not need to ask if they are still in the market. THEY WILL TELL YOU.

Take a Walk

After completing your phone calls, you need to get up and stretch, right? It is imperative you know your inventory. Take a few minutes, daily, and look at what you have to sell. If you sell an intangible product, make

a list of products you have not researched lately. Look for new items that have been delivered recently. Do you know about each one? Professional salespeople rarely have occasion to say **"Oh, gosh. That would have been perfect for Mr. and Mrs. Buyer. I wish I had known it was here."**
Your "inventory walk" has an additional purpose. Look at your inventory. If you notice something wrong with the packing, the display or the product itself bring it to the attention of management. Nothing is more difficult to overcome during the sales process than an item that is not ready to be sold.

ACTIVITY BREEDS ACTIVITY

For as long as you are in business you will hear this. Every daily activity you perform will lead to other activity. Be active at your place of business, in your sales territory or on the telephone. Look at the common traits winners exhibit <u>daily.</u>

IF YOU WERE THE GREATEST ACTOR IN THE WORLD AND NEVER GOT A PART IN A PLAY, WHO WOULD KNOW? GET IN FRONT OF PEOPLE. SELLING IS A NUMBERS GAME.

OVERCOMING OBJECTIONS

Before you learn about overcoming objections lets define what they are.

ANYTHING YOUR CUSTOMER OFFERS AS A REASON NOT TO BUY IS AN OBJECTION.

Easy enough to understand, right? To overcome them, you must understand the reason why customers offer them up and how to minimize them. Will you sell everyone if you learn this? No. That just isn't the real world.

What you CAN DO is make it easier for your customer to say YES.

When do most people learn to answer an objection?.

When the result of their effort is *NO SALE*, then they scratch their head and wonder why.

The light bulb comes on and you figure out what you should have done to overcome it. If you are currently employed in sales, I know this has happened to you. By then, it's too late. Someone else got the business. What is the best way to keep this from happening to you?

FIRST YOU MUST UNDERSTAND THE OBJECTION.

There are millions of objections. How can I possibly figure out a way of overcoming every one of them?
Think for a moment. Are there really millions of objections? There might be a million ways to say things, but there are very few objections that don't belong under just a few headings. Before we go further, don't think I am going to ask you to write down thousands of objections and ways of overcoming them. You don't have time, and you wouldn't do it anyway.

Here is what I will ask you to do. Write down the last 5 objections you heard. Just 5. Now, one at a time lets analyze your list. Since you are there, and I am here, I am going to make up a list for you.

- "The price is too high"
- "I don't like the color
- "I can't afford that"
- "I need it sooner than that"
- "It looks too complicated for me to use"

At first glance they appear to be 5 different objections. Are they? **NO.** You are hearing one objection. You are just hearing it 5 different ways.

Here is the objection:

There is something about price, product, affordability, terms of delivery or ease of use you have neglected to address.

I cannot think of many more things a customer could say that wouldn't fall into this category. So, what now?

Restate the objection in the form of a question. This will insure you are certain that what they said is what they meant.

Let's take number 1 from the list above.

The price is too high. Here is what you ask:

"It sounds to me like the only thing keeping us from

earning your business is the price, is that correct?"

If the answer is YES you can now address the objection. "If the price were $$$ would you consider going ahead and doing business now?" There might be a yes, a maybe, I might have to think it over. Guess what...do the same thing again. Restate in the form of a question and keep asking.

I recently read a book on negotiating and it took the author 6 pages to say that. Please consider this short exercise as my gift to you.

You must do this using your personal style of speech. If you don't you will sound like you are reading a script. With those words of caution, practice until you are comfortable.

5 Decisions People make Before They Buy

1. NEED OR WANT- The need buying decision is based on a change in conditions. You purchase something because you have a need for the benefit of the product. You need to cut a tree. You get a saw. You need a better way to keep track of your inventory...you get a software program. You have another child. You need a bigger vehicle.

A want decision is based on ego. You want it because it will make you feel better, impress the neighbors or help you. You want a bigger house. You want the latest electronic equipment. You want a bigger diamond, right ladies? This decision isn't because you need it, you want it.

2. BRAND-Manufacturers spend billions of dollars to advertise and promote both product and brand identity. Purchasers, in many instances, are extremely brand loyal and have made the brand decision prior to the actual shopping experience.

3. WHEN- This decision is based on lifestyle factors. I don't think people in Minnesota acquire lots of outdoor furniture in January. Have you noticed how many businesses that sell hard goods have big sales around income tax refund season? Your local car dealer advertises the heck out of vans right before summer vacation season. You get the point. There are events that trigger buying activity. Be aware of them and increase your business.

4. PRICE TO PAY- Within reason most folks know what price range the product they want falls in. They look for comparable shop prices on the internet. Look in the newspaper and watch television.

5. WHERE TO BUY- The reputation you and your company have established will guide customers to your business. The location of your business has a great deal to do with where people purchase. Don't you like the convenience of the store near your home? Your dry cleaners? The coffee shop you visit on the way to the office?

You will have customers come to your place of business due to location. They will come back and do repeat business if you **take care of them** in the proper manner. Look at these survey results from people who buy.

Do you sell most of your goods on the internet?

These same decisions apply to you as well. People want to do business where it's easy. They want a good product. They want the best price. They have a want or need. **They want to do business with someone who has a good reputation**. Is your website up to par? Do you have a compelling message? Does your content grab the reader's attention? If the answer is yes, congratulations. If your internet business isn't generating the kind of revenue you hope for the answer might be here.

Sales Training

FEATURE-FUNCTION-BENEFIT SELLING

What is it? What does it do? Why should I have it ?

What sales training information would be complete without telling you about this powerful tool? The heading above is about the most clinical definition of Feature-Function-Benefit selling I have found. Let's refer to it as FFB shall we? Mastering selling isn't easy. Using FFB during your product presentation will insure you include the most important features as they relate to your customer.

What exactly does that mean?

It means that you know what is important to your customer. You know how your product will work for them. Now it is simply a matter of presenting the product. Part of your sales training, Step 4, dealt with sharing your knowledge with enthusiasm. Imagine the impact it will have when you use FFB each step of the way.

Make FFB the Foundation of Your Presentation

It's simple to ask what is it, what does it do and why should I have it. Learning to think that way is another matter.

Let's use an example. Suppose you were an automobile salesperson. They are in a very competitive industry; it seems like there is a dealership on every corner. They all have the same basic product to sell. It has glass, wheels, an engine, etc. Now, suppose you were shopping for a new car. You are dealing with a person who has gone through extensive sales training. The salesperson says to you, this car has anti-lock brakes. Not very inspiring wording, is it? The car is SUPPOSED to have anti-lock brakes.

But what if the salesperson said, "This vehicle is equipped with an anti-lock braking system. In the event of an emergency situation, simply depress the brake pedal to the floor. A computer will prevent the wheels from locking and forcing you into a skid. You can maintain control and maybe even avoid a head-on collision if you slide into oncoming traffic. That is an important safety feature, wouldn't you agree?"

WOW

Same feature but look at the difference in how the product presentation was handled. I don't know about you, but after that, I would never buy a car that didn't have anti-lock brakes.

Use FFB to Sell Your Product

There is no item for sale that cannot be presented in this fashion. Think about the products you sell and how easy it would be to tell everyone about them in this manner.

FACT FINDING

Fact finding is gathering information by asking not only the right questions but asking them the right way.

Information about your customer, their lifestyle, their desires, needs and wants is essential.

Of the sales steps none is more important.

Do the right job here. When the time comes to ask for the business, you will be amazed at how easy it is to get a YES.

Knowledge is Power. For many years sales trainers and sales managers have called this step "qualifying", and by doing so, have done a serious disservice to their salespeople.

The word "qualify" makes you think of the dollars and cents part of the sale. How much they can they afford, how much they will pay.

Slow down. Learn what you need to know by asking **open-ended questions.**

These types of questions require a response other than "Yes" or "No".
"Do you like green?" will not get the same response as ***"What is your favorite color?"*** (When you get really good at this you will drive your friends nuts.)

Here are a few thought starters...the list is almost limitless.

- Who will be the primary user/driver/operator?

- How often, how many miles, how will you use it?

- When do you need to buy/lease/purchase?

- What do you like/dislike about the one you have now?

We could go on and on, but you get the idea. The answers you receive to the questions in Step 2 will identify the needs and wants of your customer. This makes your job easier when you know you have not only answered the questions they have asked, you know the answers to the questions you have asked.

It is important to do a good job in the second step on the road to a sale. Settling a customer on the wrong product is a recipe for disaster.

Learn from football players

Football players. What does that have to do with sales?
How can a professional athlete teach me how to sell?
Unless they have an off-season job in sales, it's probably
not much.

Here is what you can learn...

The value of practice.

People familiar with American football know the regular
season starts in September and ends in January. What

they may not know is training camps start in July. It takes time to prepare for the upcoming season. That is what I want to talk to you about. This will require some simple arithmetic so don't panic...we can work through this together.

You know training camp starts in July. The season starts in September. That allows about 8 weeks for training. If the team trains 6 days a week that is 48 days of training. Let's assume it's about an 8-hour training day. 48 days of training multiplied by 8 hours per day equals 384 hours of training. By the way, most players train in the off season as well.

Now let's talk about the season itself. The regular season is 16 games. A game has four quarters that last 15 minutes each. That is one hour of actual playing time. Which means **the entire season can be played in 16 hours!**

For those of you not familiar with football as it is played in America the team consists of an offense and a defense. Very few players, if any, play both. Which means their playing time is only 8 hours per season if they play every play. So, you know how much the player practiced, 384 hours. You know how much he plays during the season, 8 hours. **For every hour of playing time he practiced 48 hours.**
How much do you practice? Is it any wonder you are not improving? Let's do the arithmetic on your "season".

You work 5 days a week? 8 hours a day? How much of that time is spent in a face to face selling situation? The rest of your time is driving to appointments, doing paperwork, staying organized, and doing follow ups. Determine how much time you spend in front of customers. It may surprise you how little it is. The point here is simple...practice like a football player so when your "playing time" comes you will be prepared.

PRE-OWNED FORMAT INFO CALL

Sell the appointment

1. Hello_____ speaking. How can I help you?
After customer identifies needs) You picked a great time to call us!

1a. We've been selling so many cars recently with all the new promotions we've had going on, and as a result we've been taking in plenty of trades. Not only_____ but other vehicles like them as well.

2. What year range were you considering?

Would you also consider a year newer, as well if it fit in the budget?

Stay away from price ranges, colors and mileage requirements.)

Aside from _____'s, are there any other models you would consider if they met your requirements?

This isn't something you have to do right away, is it?

3. Great! Let me do this for you. I'm going to check not only what we have available now in _____'s but also what we have coming on trade in the next few days as well. It shouldn't take me very long at all.

Are you calling from home or work?

What's your number there?

Your last name?

Your first name?

In case I miss you at that number, what's your cell phone number?

Could you hold for just a moment?

4. I just checked and as I indicated earlier, we've been selling so many new cars recently we have no shortage of pre-owned vehicles. Your biggest challenge here won't be finding a vehicle, it will be narrowing it down to just one! By the way, what are you currently driving?

Is that the vehicle you would consider trading in? Begin qualifying the trade.

5. When would be a good time for us to get together? Would later today be good or would this evening be better?

How does sound? If customer hesitates or is uncertain of specific time: (most likely what time do you think it might be?)

Great! I'm going to pencil you in my calendar for _____. If for any reason your running a little early or late, would you please call me so I can adjust my schedule?

6. Do you have a pen and paper handy?

Write down my name. My last name is spelled _____ and my first name is _____.

Just remember, what you're trying to accomplish here is to set an appointment and to sell the appointment. Unless you're selling this car on eBay or somehow over the Internet in your shipping it out a state or overseas, you want this customer to show up either at your franchised dealership or at your independent use car lot as soon as possible. You can't push that car through the phone and get it to the customer unless it's a straight Internet deal.

Selling and setting the appointment is the absolute most important thing you could do over the phone. You must control the conversation. If the customer controls the conversation, you lose, and they win. If you control the conversation, you will avoid talking about price and specifics, set the appointment and sell the appointment. The customer will show up and you have a very strong chance of selling that car. If you give the customer all the information over the phone, then they have absolutely no reason to show up at your dealership for any reason.

Let's face the facts, if they are ready have all the information from you about a specific vehicle there calling on, why do they need to come there if they're still in the shopping mode? Now, you gave him all the information that they're looking for, and they could go somewhere else. Most of the time while people looking for cars, they end up buying something other than what they came for. Often, they might find something else on your lot they weren't thinking about; it could be a new car that hasn't been advertised that they could fall in love with and end up buying.

That's why selling and setting the appointment be your priority on the phone. Your number one priority should be to get the customer into the dealership. By following this process and sticking to the script, you will have a great chance of success achieving all the of the above goals. Remember the path that you're leading them down is to stop talking about price, payment, color, but getting them to do it your way.

And when I say to begin qualifying the trade, let them sell you their car. After all, that's what their intentions are. Find out the year, make, model, miles, and condition. The more they talk about their car, the less they will want it.

CREDIT CHALLENGE PHONE-UP FORMAT

Individuals with specific credit challenges (bankruptcy, repossession, and slow pay) constitute a large percentage of the buying public today. By not recognizing and capitalizing on this fact, you will severely limit your opportunities.

Treat these customers with respect and always remember they represent as big or bigger commission in many cases than that person with "gold" credit. Do not over qualify on the telephone. This can be insulting. People are more apt to feel comfortable and open up when sitting down with you face to face.

The biggest key to remember is they, like you, want a car they can be happy with. Don't lose that focus by centering your conversation around phone bills, proof of income, proof of birth, down payment, etc. They called for a car! By treating everyone with respect and dignity you'll find yourself delivering a lot more vehicles!

SALESPERSON: Hello, this is _____ speaking. How can I help you?

CUSTOMER: I want to know if you can help me get financed...

SALESPERSON: I'm glad you called us. Our dealership specializes in challenges like yours. We work with a number of different lending institutions, probably more than any other dealership in the area. Because of that, we can overcome many obstacles most other dealerships can only imagine. What type of vehicle were you considering?

CUSTOMER: A _____.

SALESPERSON: (continue and lead right into the phone script.)

Just remember these are the best customers you can get. Somebody with perfect credit is going to sit there negotiate with you for hours and days. However, somebody who has substandard credit just wants to drive a car and be happy with what they bought. They want to have a good solid finance package put together for them. These folks are the ones you make money on, and that's capitalism. So, when somebody calls you starting out the conversation this way, you probably just sold a vehicle. More than that, you probably just got a good customer for life. So, treat them with respect. Take very good care of them because they're going to come back to you to buy a second vehicle.

PHONE-UP FORMAT NEW CARS

1. Hello, this is _____ speaking. How can I help you?

(After prospect identifies needs) You picked a great time to call us on 's._____(MODEL LINE)

P: With your permission, I'd like to ask you a couple questions regarding _____you're considering.

A: That way you'll know we're both talking about the same vehicle.

C: Would that be o.k.?

2. How familiar are you with the _____?

Are you looking for that in the _____?

2 or 4 wheel drive?

4 or 6 cylinder?

Manual or automatic? Light or dark color?

Have you had an opportunity to drive the yet?

This isn't something you have to do right away, is it?

3. Great! Let me do this for you. I'm going to check not only what we have available now in _____ 's, but also what we have incoming. It shouldn't take me very long at all.

Are you calling from home or work?

What's your number there?

Your last name?

Your first name?

In case I miss you at that number, what's your cell phone number?

Could you hold for just a moment?

4. I just checked, and we have a great availability of_____ 's right now. By the way, are you currently an_____ owner?

What are you driving? Is that the vehicle you would consider trading in? (Begin qualifying the trade.)

5. When would be a good time for us to get together? Would later today be good or would this evening be better?

How does sound? If prospect hesitates or is uncertain of specific time: most likely what time do you think it might be?

Great! I'm going to pencil you in my calendar for
_____. If for any reason you're running a little early or
late would you please call me so I can adjust my schedule?

6. Do you have a pen and paper handy?

Write down my name. My last name is spelled, and my first
name is _____.

.

Again, like I stated in the last section, you're here to control the
conversation and sell and set the appointment. Not to try to sell
the vehicle over the phone and like I said before a lesser sell in
this vehicle on eBay or different online source, you want to sell
and set the appointment and get the customer into your
dealership above all. This script is your game plan; it is how
you're going to win and sell more cars whether you're an
independent or franchise dealership. One of the best sources
for good solid phone training that I would highly recommend
would be Alan Ram with proactive phone training solutions. I
believe their website is proactive training solutions.com, this is
by far the most superior phone training scripts and solutions if
you're an independent or franchise dealership. In fact, if you're
a franchise dealership, you should sign up with this company
ASAP because I strongly believe there isn't a better phone
training solution out there.

SOCIAL MEDIA

1. Facebook
2. Instagram
3. Craigslist
4. Google
5. AdWords/ Google
6. YouTube

These six formats of social media are something that we can't live without. The average person spends nine hours a day on some form of social media. Just think about this for a second, there is 8 hours in a work day and 40 hours a week during a common work week. So, we spend more time on social media than we do at our actual jobs. So, as far as advertising is concerned, what better format do you have than talking to people who are a captive audience.

Facebook has turned out to be one of the best sources as far as advertising. However, you have to be careful to make sure that you're not just trying to sell things; you're trying to create a presence. A presence should be fun, engaging, and full of information. You want to create something that people are going to want to watch and engage with. It's not all about likes; followers and engagement are key. Most of the time you want to create a one-minute video. Usually you can go a little bit longer, but I would recommend staying at a maximum video time of two minutes. Anything beyond that mark is when you usually lose the person's attention.

So, let's just take this for example. You're advertising a car for sale at your dealership. So, what you want to do is talk about what's special about that car, and what's special about the deal. You want to tell somebody why they should come to you and buy that vehicle. The engagement should be fun and lighthearted, not serious. You don't want to be pressing or forceful by pushing the narrative that you have to buy this today or the world is going to blow up.

The less you push something, the more people are going to want to buy it. Remember, you have a captive audience here. They're spending nine hours a day on social media, and it's very easy for them to scroll away from something if it isn't engaging. Now, there's one other thing you can do is boost the post. This method costs money, but the amount of money it costs to boost a post is pennies compared to any other source. You also want to do Facebook marketplace. You're advertising your car on Facebook marketplace, and you can do up to 10 groups at a time. These groups are categories that you can use to advertise your product.

This is a little time-consuming, but it is worth it because people will engage with you through Instant Messenger or directly on your Facebook site. Yes, you should have all your advertisement on your personal Facebook site as well as the dealerships. You want to invite all of your friends. Ideally, you want any and all of your contacts to go like and follow your Facebook page.

One of the other things you want to do on Facebook is do short information updates like what's happening with the dealership or something that's going on in the community. You want to post about events or community involved causes with the police or fire department or local military. Pets for adoption is also a great way to engage with the community. You want to show that you care and are giving back to the community.

These kind of community events is what's going to build up the trust and respect level on Facebook with the community where you going to evolve to have frequent followers and watchers of your videos and your messages of what you have to say this will legitimize you and set you apart from everybody else that's posting, sales etc.

Also, Facebook has an inventory tab. So, depending on who your DMS provider is, you can push your inventory directly into Facebook marketplace. You don't want to do this as a blanket push; what you want to do is do it individually. Maybe try one every two hours, and hand write out a partial description what's special about it and what you have to offer. Do not be repetitive about the same special or the same vehicle. If you really want to push something, do a boost post.

INSTAGRAM:

This social media platform is quickly becoming a very strong vessel to do your advertisement in. Now, it's got to be brief to the point. This is where hashtags are very important. Some of the most widely used hashtags are love, beauty, popular, your website. This is strictly video or 1 to 5 pictures if you use the add designer from Instagram. You can easily gain a lot of followers. Do cross posting between Facebook and Instagram as this is something that should go together. Instagram has multiple platforms that you can take full advantage of. Just making sure your posts are relevant, brief, and to the point.

For example, if you want to advertise a particular vehicle, all you have to do is post a picture or less than one-minute video of the vehicle. In the description area again, being short and sweet say what it is, and what you're doing, and fill it with hashtags that are all relevant to you and your business. You want to add in the "love" and the "beauty" hashtag because those are two of the most popular hashtags on Instagram. Gaining followers is a very important thing. The more followers you have, the more widely you are seen between Facebook and Instagram. Your social media presence will increase because of this. If you're always shooting video every single day 2-3 times a day, even some that are not necessarily selling anything, you are going to gain followers. Invite people to like it. The more you put into this, the more you're going to get out of it.

Instagram also has a promote feature which again is pennies on the dollar. So, all of your important posts should be promoted through their recommendations button. Their promotions button works excellent along with Facebook, and it will get you really good results. You can either drive people to your website or get click throughs, and you want to do the click throughs to your website.

They will also provide you analytics data at the end of each promotion. Just like Facebook, this will be data on the performance and outcome of what your promotion did. Normally, I would do this for a seven-day package. If your results are very good, you might want to boost it and re-promote it on both formats. You can pick a different geographical location if you wanted to. Don't get too specific on age range. I always pick the 18 to 65, and don't worry about whether it's men or women. It really doesn't matter. Your geographic location, however, does matter. Basically, this is like geo-fencing. Think about it for a second. Think how far you would travel to go buy a car or any type of product for that matter that you must go and pick up. I would say most car dealerships would be okay staying within a 250-mile radius. So geo-fence yourself within 250 miles. You can do less entirely, but that's my recommendation.

The days of doing ZIP Code search for advertising purposes are pretty much dead. Now, if you ended up being lucky enough to get the cross-sell report, or a whole data report to show you in your ZIP Code what is selling this will break down the year make and models of the vehicles, which is very strong good information, which will talk about later in this book. But this is where the part of geo-fencing comes in you can take your ZIP Code and go out a minimum of 50 miles and I suggest a maximum of 250 miles.

CRAIGSLIST:

Craigslist is by far the best medium to advertise cars in the marketplace. Craigslist receives over 1 billion hits on their website every single month. It is the number one website out of any website that there is. I would post on Craigslist and get any type of posting service that does a good job that makes it look personal to post as many ads as possible on Craigslist daily. Posting to multiple cities is a difficult thing to do with Craigslist, but it can be done. I would take at least 15 up to their maximum of 24 pictures of the vehicle and a very good and solid description of the vehicle each add.

The title is the absolute most important one. Make sure you only capitalize each letter in the sentence and not the entire word because you will end up getting flagged by Craigslist. In the location field you can put your website or any snippet that you can think of. One of the things you definitely want to do is add keywords to the bottom of the ad. These are words such as Ford, Chevy, Dodge, Toyota, Honda, etc. Make sure to fill in every single field including the list price, phone number and email.

Now, there's been a lot of hype about Craigslist with personal ads, and all kinds of other negative reactions that people have when coming to the site. But, I can tell you from personal experience that there is nothing better that you could possibly advertise on than this website. I don't care what you're selling or what you're trying to achieve, if you post it, you will get a response. If you're smart about your geo-fencing, you can post to multiple cities with the same ad and get an incredible response almost immediately.

 The one thing about posting to multiple cities is that you do have to change some of the content and some of the title in the ad otherwise Craigslist will pick it up and flagged the ad. Flagging the ad basically will turn your post pink in your online portal which means the ad has been removed. There are a lot of posting services out there which you must be careful of because they will make your ads look generic and have very little effect.

Your ads have to be personal and professional. They have to have more than a couple words in the body. In addition, there needs to be a description of the vehicle and a positive couple of sentences from you that are personal. An example of this would be, "This car runs great! Gets great gas mileage, smells new looks new, and has no issues. Has been nothing but reliable transportation for me!" Things like this will get you noticed and will get you lots of phone calls.

I would try and post my entire inventory every single day seven days a week on Craigslist. If you're not capable of posting your entire inventory every day, I would at least take out the top 5 to 10 vehicles. Make sure that they're posted every day. Yes, this is time-consuming and tedious work, but will absolutely sell you a lot of cars.

GOOGLE:

When it comes to search engine optimization search engine marketing promoting your business promoting yourself any type of website or any type of advertising source whatsoever, Google dominates the entire market. There are many books programs, classes, lectures, workshops, that you can take to figure out where your niches geo-fence yourself and get on the Google program. Whether you're doing PPC, which stands for pay per click. Or you are doing ad words display ads video ads network ads organic SEO or SEM, if you don't sign up and get everything Google has to offer you will lose.

Google has some very important intense programs. They have some great information and educational programs that will help you promote your website, your inventory, and anything else that you're doing. It is imperative that you get familiar with this and not just hand it over to some marketing company. All they will do will is take your money, and you will get very little or low results.

Google analytics is something you want tied into your website and your business. This is one source that you can look up even from the Google mobile app and see how you're doing daily. Trust me, this will surprise you. You can also get this from being on Yahoo, but the reality is that Google dominates. My advice to you is to stay away from Yelp. This source really isn't going to help you in any way, so don't even worry about it. Getting Google reviews and likes will be one of the most important things that you can do. We will get into likes and reviews later, but this is an area that again is imperative that you participate.

Everybody talks about getting on the first page. Even though this is greatly important, what's more important is that you come up in the search that's relevant to what you're doing. For example, let's say you're selling a used car, if somebody does a used car search even though you may be a top advertiser it is not a guarantee that you would come up under this particular search even though you may be in the business. So, when you do broad match applications, this is something that should guarantee you coming up on the first page when somebody is doing the search for used car in your area.

Google has many different platforms that are extremely important. Just look at their programs, take it one by one, and do the best you can to learn them all or least get yourself very familiar with what's going on. If you do decide to hire somebody, you will have some type of educational background, so you can talk intelligently with the person that's going to be doing your Google marketing.

ADWORDS:

Google ad words is basically Google's platform for PPC. If you have a website and you're hoping to sell vehicles, whether you're working for a dealership or not, this is something that you could spend a minimum of $20 a day. There really is no maximum whatsoever. The more money you spend in this area of ad words the more traffic you're going to get to your website the more cars are going to sell the more of everything is coming your way, in this platform the person with the biggest wallet wins.

There are multiple facets in the ad words game that will help you directly drive traffic to your business or personal website to help you sell cars and make money if you can afford to invest $1500 a month into this platform as a single person working for dealership or if you have your own this is definitely the way to go. You absolutely will not lose. Google has training programs online through them for free that you can get yourself Google certified and add word certified. In fact, there are several books out there that I would purchase and make that personal investment in one of them is card dog millionaire written by Jim Flynt. And googleopoly written by Shawn Bradley. Both books have different views but are equally as good. Either way get yourself involved in the ad words game the sooner the better.

There's a lot of Internet books out there it doesn't hurt to read a bunch and get as much education in the digital media world as possible this can only help you and will enhance your business. And if you're looking to enhance your phone skills a good program is the late Alan Rams proactive training solutions, and Dealer retention services also has a very good program.

YOUTUBE:

Everything starts with YouTube, the first thing you need to do is set up a YouTube channel make sure it's professional clean looking and simple. All the videos that you going to make me need to do through YouTube this way the URL once you place it on Facebook or anywhere else all resorts back to YouTube where you house everything that's basically, your basis. You can track your analytics, your data your views click likes content everything is trackable through YouTube via Google analytics. You can then promote your YouTube channel throughout all your social media and any other content that you desire.

The biggest thing that will happen with your YouTube channel is getting subscribers. These are people who were frequently engage in watcher channel which will all turn into potential customers. The biggest thing about YouTube is to make sure you're filling it with content that is desirable to your audience. Especially in the car business we have many facets where you can fill your channel up with content just think of how many how to videos you can make with all the product knowledge that you have.

For example, let's take a late-model navigation system pretty much from any manufacturer you can simply do a how-to video just on this alone. You could do a how-to video even as something simple like changing a tire and believe it or not the way some of the new tires are mounted on these late model vehicles actually can be a little complicated and if you're not sure how to do it your video could be extremely useful and end up with a lot of subscribers just because of that one. There are just endless possibilities of things you can do with YouTube that'll be productive and profitable.

Just remember make sure your content is clean simple to the point educational impact with information, this will keep your subscribers coming back to you over and over again and when it's time for them to buy a car sell a car you want them to feel comfortable to get in contact with you so you're at the top of their list for buying purposes.

CLOSING SKILLS

There are probably over 100 different unique skills when it comes to closing a deal. There are all kinds of books and sales trainers out there that'll give you their 101 basic closing skills. Now, you could read all the books from all the greats like Grant Cardone, Joe Verde, Zig Ziglar, and many others that are in the industry. But none of their techniques will help you unless you overcome one thing: FEAR.

Fear is the number one killer of salespeople. It's the fear of rejection, the fear of the customer saying no, the fear of not making the sale, the fear of wasting hours of your valuable time and not making the sale. It's also the fear of upsetting a customer, or even the fear of making your managers or supervisors upset at you for not closing the deal. The thing that you want to remember is that the worst thing that your customer could say is no.

One of the things that I say all the time to a customer, to their typical response of "Well, let me think about it," My response is, "Mr. Customer, there are only three reasons why you need to think about it #1 do you like the vehicle? #2 are you okay doing business with me?, #3 are you okay with the price point?" If the person answers yes to all three, let's get you in your new vehicle.

If he answers no to any of those three objections, then you have your answer. Now, you need to fix one of the three, most likely it's not going to be the vehicle and it's not going to be the dealership or you it's going to be the price and that's where your selling comes in. If you've done a good enough job doing the basic skills of selling value instead of price than this last objection isn't going to be an issue but obviously if it is it's either going to be one of two things either this person is paying cash or he's going to make payments.

77% of all car buyers finance. This means that most likely the person you're selling a car to is either over buying if they're not signing up right away where that comes in is your vehicle selection. Because most people believe that the payment is too high, you could overcome this objection in one simple way. Look at the payment that they're paying now on their trade-in if they have one which most likely the vehicle that they have if it's an average of four years old and an average of 15,000 miles a year it's going to have about 60,000 miles which most common vehicles are going to be out of warranty so take the difference between the two payments Sophie's paying $400 a month now and the new payment of $600 a month he believes he's actually spending more money in reality he's going to be spending less here's why.

there a $200 a month payment difference. As a statistical fact every year the manufacturers get better at producing vehicles with better gas mileage so the chances are the four-year-old vehicle and the new vehicle they're looking at There is definitely a gas mileage difference which means the cost of fuel will be less which also means the cost of fuel that he's paying right now is higher so you can take that into effect. Also, since the vehicles out of warranty to average vehicle maintenance cost is $900 per year so you add 4 years that's $3600.

Then you take the average repairs which average $1600 and you add these together along with the additional fuel cost, that's a $10,000 minimal difference which comes out to $208 per month. So in reality by buying the new vehicle it's going to be cheaper for him by eight dollars a month, plus the additional fuel savings. You can slice and dice this example all you want there are many different ways to put something like this together to come out with the complete justification that a difference in $200 will actually be cheaper on a monthly payment than what that person is paying now because they're also upgrading to a vehicle with 0 miles and a full factory warranty and a full maintenance program.

Another example is that when somebody says, "Well, let me discuss it with my wife or my husband first." The reality is having you ever gone shopping for a $50 or $100,000 thousand dollar or even $20,000 item without your spouse knowing? Of course not, they are ready know where you're going, and what you're doing. So, an easy response is, "Well, if you're like me I'm sure your spouse already knows that you're here, so let's give him or her a call and let's see what they think. As a matter of fact, we do offer a free test drive. So, let's bring him or her the vehicle so they can look at it you both can make an intelligent decision together."

We have over 101 closing techniques that you can pick up from our books, websites and free YouTube videos, but we will get to a few more of these in later chapters.

Just remember closing techniques are just a system and there are many systems out there with you like ours "the national automotive training Academy" or you like Grant Cardone, Joe Verde, zig Ziglar, Tony Robbins, or just whoever. The important thing is to learn a few good techniques and become an expert at it. We all could give you many examples in many different techniques to closing the deal but until you practice it and expert it, all they are his words on a page or words that you hear.

If you've ever heard the terminology that practice makes perfect well I hate to tell you it's true. You're never going to memorize and expert over 100 different techniques on closing a deal but what you can do is take the top 10 that you're comfortable with that make the most sense to you and try to master at least 5 of those. The biggest thing to remember is that you are comfortable with them because you want to make sure that your responses do not sound canned, but they sound natural.

Just like an actor, when they study a script it's already prewritten for them by somebody else, so an actor is just saying the words that belong to somebody else but through their practice and professionalism they make it sound 100% natural. Just take one closing technique at a time practice it every day for the next 10 days say it repeatedly as many times a day as you can and practice it this way it'll come out naturally so when that objection comes up it'll just flow.

GOALS

In this section you will learn how to probably make and set goals which are probably the most important thing you can do. There's a lot to be said about goals I've read so many books about goals and achieving your goals and looking in the mirror and making sure your goals are achievable or they're not too high they're not too low, everybody seems to have an opinion on goals.

The one thing I know for sure is let's set these in mile stones, so they are achievable. That's the whole point. If you set a goal and you don't achieve it then what happens it becomes a negative, and why would you want to set something that's not within your sites and reasonable to hit now I'm not saying let's make everything easy so it's not a goal so just something you do, that's not what I'm saying. I'm saying let's set your sights on a target on a number and let's break it down and get it done.

So, let's say the goal here is to sell 25 vehicles per month. You can't just wake up one morning and sell 25 cars first you must get to 10, then 12, then 15, then 20, then 25. First you must pass every single one of these numbers before you get to the result, so let's just say the first goal is to sell 10 vehicles. How is that going to happen? Well let's do the math on it, because the math never lies.

So, reality is you're going to close 25% of your deals which is a pretty good number to stick with, in my opinion if you can close 25% really shouldn't be doing this. So, this means to sell 10 vehicles you have to have 40 solid leads. So how are you going to generate 40 solid leads to sell 10 cars. Well you're going to get this from a few different sources one is going to be your walk-in traffic, the telephone, the Internet, and self-prospecting. So, you have four sources for you to generate business let's talk about the first one your walk-in traffic.

Walk in traffic (showroom)

every store in America has walk-in traffic this is a product of the thousands of dollars that all dealerships spend every single month, so people will come to the dealership. This is the low hanging fruit and trust me I'm not saying it's bad it's great because the more ups you take and the more aggressive you are and the more polished you are on your closing skills will only sell you more cars this is where the meet and greet steps in.

The telephone

This is absolutely my favorite way of engagement with a customer. For me the telephone can be your best friend enclosed in this book is a telephone script one of the best one sent out there that was originally written by Alan Ram and proactive training solutions, if you really want to sharpen up your phone skills they have a great program for you to get into.

If you practice the phone scripts that are enclosed, and I mean really practiced them, so they come out naturally, remember like I said earlier about being an actor and studying your script? This is one great way of doing because the phone is absolutely the best source. If somebody's calling you on the phone about a vehicle that you have on your website advertised, they are a buyer. So, your job to set the appointment.

Appointments are what it's all about, everything is about setting and confirming appointments I can't stress this enough. Once you have a confirmed appointment the reality is you probably got a sale, so the number one thing you want to do is set as many appointments per day as you can from all your resources. Even if that means spending your entire day talking to people and setting appointments throughout the week and confirming them sometimes repeatedly will only ensure your success.

Appointments is absolutely the way to go and getting them confirmed is just as important. By you having a conversation with somebody over the phone gives you the opportunity to develop a relationship this is what gets you the appointment and when the customer pulls up to the dealership they already feel comfortable because the ice is already broken they feel that they know you so it's important that you have fun with them over the phone don't be robotic or strict have a conversation develop a relationship sometimes for some people this is a little bit difficult but I can tell you the reward is great and lucrative.

The Internet

The Internet is everything I've been talking about since the beginning of this book which is basically promote yourself online in every different possible media source you have access to. There are a ton of selling apps like 5-mile, like let it go, like offer up, Facebook marketplace, Craigslist. You need to promote yourself and list your vehicles on all these apps, especially if you're selling used cars, this is something you can't go without the put your face and name out there for people to know get used doing get familiar with. This is a great source to generate business.

Prospecting

Prospecting is getting yourself out of the dealership at least three days a week and go visit local businesses that are in your area. I suggest go to your local doughnut store cut a deal with them and buy yourselves a few dozen doughnuts every time you go out scotch tape your business card to lid of the box of doughnuts and go visit all these different businesses it doesn't matter what they are whether their insurance agencies, factories, the post office, hair salons, nail salons, you get the point.

Getting yourself out there in the community and make these stops introducing yourself and striking up conversations with these local business owners will only generate you more business. One thing to do is even talk to a local large company like here in Houston we have a lot of oil and gas companies and they buy lots of trucks, so one thing that we have done in the past is talk to their HR department ask if it would be okay if we set up in their lobby for an entire day, have some donuts and other snacks there at the table along with a bunch of brochures and business cards. Just sit there and wait and his people come off the elevator come through the main lobby. They will see your dealerships banner with a lot of point of sale materials and you'd be surprised on how many people will stop and talk to you.

 I have personally generated hundreds of sales that I would normally not have because of this process. This is something that you can do on multiple levels all the time, and I'm sure you'll find that the owner or general manager of your dealership won't object. in fact, they may encourage it. So instead of hanging around with all your friends at the dealership be productive and do your outside prospecting.

One other good thing to do in prospecting is make sure you always have business cards on you and everybody you meet give them your business card you should go through a box of 500 business cards every month if you're not you're not doing enough, and this is the minimum.

Prospecting is nothing more than cultivating your business because that's exactly what this is you have your own business inside of a business so just think about what you would do if your name was on the building it's basically the same principle why would it be any different.

The dealership provides you with the inventory and office space for you to have a million-dollar career. So, invest in yourself and go out in prospect everywhere you can, the Internet is just not enough advertising is just not enough it's that one-on-one personal contact to shake somebody's hand look them in the eye and be able to do business with them the old-fashioned way. People would like nothing more than to have a friend in the car business and you can be exactly that.

INVEST IN YOUR SELF

The greatest book ever written is the Bible. Whether you're religious or not makes a difference one of the basic principles in life itself is the one principal that God said if you build your foundation upon a rock it will stand for all time, if you build your foundation upon sand it will crumble before it ever gets finished. There is no basic principle in life that has had any truer meaning.

The first one is financial responsibility or as some people say your financial mindset. Essentially, get your money right first. This means control your personal finances at home and make sure you're 100% solvent before you try and do anything else. It means know your budget, know your goals for your own household, and know how much it cost you to go to work every day. For example, let's just say your total monthly bills food, car payment, rent, electric, all your essentials cost you $3000 a month to live.

This means based upon a 27-day work month which is what the average is it would cost you $111 per day for you to go to work before you make one dollar for yourself. So, in other words every day you wake up and go to work it cost you $111 to show up, so if you went to work and you sold the car and you made $250 that one day on that one sale that means for that day you made $138 profit. You covered your cost and made a profit based on that rate you would cover your cost and make a $3750 profit that month. This is what it means to get your money right know where you're at hundred percent of the time.

So now what happens when you go to work, and you don't do what you're supposed to do, and you don't sell a car? What happens is you go into the negative. For example, you showed up to work on Monday and you didn't sell a car now you show up Tuesday and your $222 is your cost for that day the show up to work because you didn't sell a car on Monday.

Let each day stand on its own hopefully if you go two or three days without selling a vehicle and then you do so one and it's a really big deal the same principle applies you monist your cost factor out of your total commission that you made on that deal and hopefully you're at a positive or at least a breakeven let's hope that you're at a positive.

Getting full 100% control of your personal finances at home is absolutely a very important thing to do. Having full control of this will give you superior confidence when you walk out of your house walk into your business and know you're going to make the day pay.

FOLLOW UP

Do you realize that 25% of all salespeople make the first phone call on a follow-up situation? 48% never even get to the second phone call and over 70% never make a phone call even after that. Statistics show that it takes between six and 12 follow-up phone calls to close a customer. So, your closing skills can be great but if you don't follow up and be persistent you're never going to get the sale somebody else will.

Follow-up is the number one killer of salespeople and dealerships, I can't stress this enough when I tell you your follow up with a customer is imperative. You need to set out from the beginning knowing that once the customer leaves your dealership or breaks a confirmed appointment that it's going to take you somewhere between six and 12 times of follow-up phone calls emails and text messages to get that customer to come in.

What I like to do is to set a schedule for that customer if the customer left my dealership in the morning I'm going to give them a phone call that evening, then they're going to receive an informational email and a text message from me all over the next 72 hours. In this process will repeat itself until the customer tells me to please stop contacting them or comes in and buys a vehicle. Never let a lead out of your sight always understand that that customer that you spoke with is a solid prospect that you do have a relationship with and to let that fall by the wayside because of laziness or non-persistence is a crime.

A lot of people these days respond mainly to text messages so one thing you should do is take a picture with your phone of your business card and send it to that prospect. The next thing is to send them possibly an "E brochure" or an email that's dedicated to the information on the product they were looking at with you. And of course, the best thing is to pick up the phone and call them even if you must leave a message. Another great thing that you can do right off your phone is due a short 30 SECOND video. And just basically say "Hi Mr. and Mrs. Jones, it was great meeting with you the other day. Thank you for the opportunity for me to show you our great product. I just wanted to follow up with you and see if there's any questions you still had left that I can answer or anything that I can do for you, I look forward to hearing from you, once again here's my phone number and email address. Please feel free to contact me at any time."

A lot of times I would just send the video write to their cell phone and let them know it's coming from you so once you send a video tag it and say this is from your friend John Doe at ABC motors. Just remember to follow up every single day that should be the first thing you do when you come into your office in the morning. Make sure you set aside that time every single morning to do it unless you have a customer. If you sold the car first thing that's awesome; that's the goal. After that, don't forget it's time for follow-up.

WRITE UP A DEAL

Write up a deal? Of course everybody wants to write up a deal, what I mean by that is even if you have not sat down with somebody, let's say somebody made an appointment with you and didn't show up and now you're having trouble getting them back on the phone or back in contact with you, what you should do is go right up a deal, Then email the deal, the worst thing that they could say is no. or at least you'll get a confirmed answer as to why you're getting stonewalled, but putting something down on paper and writing something up makes it real.

So, just write up a deal. Now let's just say you with the customer that you met on the lot and as you are walking back into the dealership they start thanking you for your time and they want to think about it, they're not sure. It's very easy to say, Mr. customer did you happen to like this vehicle? They're either going to say yes or no and let's just say they said yes.

Say great tell you what just give me five more minutes of your time and let's just look at some of the numbers let me write up a deal for you, so you have something to think about. Now what this does, is it starts to bring that vehicle into reality for that customer. so now let's just say they're telling you that they think it's expensive or unaffordable, by you putting it down on paper and writing up a deal it starts to become real. so now you can go over some facts and some figures especially if they like the car.

Now you can start working the numbers with them, as you start to discuss It, they start look at the numbers, Mr. Customer, what were you thinking of mostly, payment or price. What did you have in mind? are you paying cash, or you are financing? hopefully those questions will be something you're ready asked when you did your research. by putting this on paper a lot stronger chance of closing the deal. I have never closed the customer without writing up a deal first.

Writing up a deal is the only surefire way to change somebody from kicking tires, looking around to purchasing a vehicle. Once they see that the vehicle they're looking at is very affordable and they're getting a great deal were getting a great payment most of the time this is the swaying decision.

Don't kid yourself it's all about the math. Customers don't want to be disrespectful to you so instead they'll tell you a story make up some great excuses, because they don't do this every day, you do. So you are the professional that's why you have to bring them along, because they are subject to passing on a deal because in their mind it's unaffordable when you and I both know you can make it affordable, customers will bend, the dealership will bend, and somewhere in the middle were going to meet and make a deal and you're going to gain a customer, hopefully for life.

So, write up every single deal!

TRAINING

In my 30-year career I have heard every single excuse in the book when it comes to training. I have a good friend of mind that's been selling cars consistently and successfully for about 15 years. This guy hates to train. He has threatened to quit several times if we make him go to different training seminars, and we have had some knockdown drag out fights and arguments about it, but he completely refuses.

Now he's a very talented good salesperson that consistently sells between 12 and 15 cars every single month and he's been doing it for years and he always says I'm consistent, and the most consistent in the dealership, I sell 15 cars every month why I need to go to training. This is exactly why you need the training because if a person can be consistently selling 12 to 15 cars every single month without training, just imagine what you could do if you had some good new training techniques. Sales techniques change daily in our industry.

Just imagine a football team just imagine what a disaster would be if they didn't practice or trained every single day. because that's what professionals do, all professionals train every single day. take a superior athlete like Michael Phelps who has two dozen gold medals, do you seriously think that he hasn't trained every single day to be on the top of his game, to be the best of the best.

Or a guy like Tiger Woods there is a guy who trained every single day of his life, his adolescent life and his adult life, and look at him he's one of the best golfers the world has ever seen. do you think he got that way by not training of course not? Now look at yourself, you decided to become a professional salesperson you're in one of the best jobs, one of the best industries in the world.

Oh, and by the way the grass is not greener on the other side. Dealerships are dealerships, stay put and train. If you're not doing well at the store you're at now what makes you think by going to another dealership it's going to be any better? You're still taking you with you, so you're going to take the same problems in the same issues to the next store. So, what's the point, like I said just stay put in train and be the best at the store you're at.

If you're going to be a professional automotive salesperson you need to train every day, every day you need to make yourself better than you were the day before. that's phone training, that's walk arounds, that's demos, that's all different skills, I would go to every seminar that you can go to, and I would read every book that you can get your hands on. I would make sure I would attend every event that your manufacturer puts on and train.

If you can train seven days a week I would suggest you do it. This needs to be part of your routine and part of your daily practice. there are tons of videos and trainers on YouTube, you can do it 45 minutes a day doesn't matter if you do something every day to better yourself. You will then become a professional salesperson because the last thing you want to do is become average.

Professional salesperson sells more than 25 cars a month, you need to be one of these people. You don't want to sell an average of 12 to 15 cars, you want to be better every single month. You want to increase every month to sell at least 25 cars a month and make the big bucks and have everything that life has to offer. If you stay strong on your follow-up skills, your training skills, you will be successful. You will be number one at your dealership; it would be inevitable. So, the only thing I can tell you is you need to grab every bit of training you can and don't ever stop. Don't ever think that you don't have anything else to learn because you're wrong. You do need it now, all the time, every day.

Along with our great training program that we have to offer which is online and in person. Here are some of the few that I trust, and I think bringing an extreme amount of value to the table. Grant Cardone, dealer retention services, Alan Ramm proactive training solutions, zig Ziglar.

One thing you must do is remember that training is exactly that it's training. Without it would be impossible to be successful. I had a conversation with a salesperson once who told me he was the best of the best and he didn't need any training. I was running a dealership at this time and I had set up a two-day seminar with a sales training company that was going to train my staff over a couple of days.

Kind of like a refresher course on the basics and follow-up and a lot of the things that I've talked about in this book. So, we had a conversation me and Jim, he said that he needed to get off early that day because he had to bring his son to football practice. I said Jim, why does he need to go to practice for he's already on the team isn't the game Friday night? Jim looked at me and said Don you out of your mind he has practice at high school every single day, and yes, the game is Friday night.

I said Jim, why would you need to bring him to practice every single day when he's already made the team, and the games are ready set for the rest of the year, every Friday night. I don't understand why he needs to practice. He looked at me like I was crazy, are you serious, you think he's going to go to the game and not practice every day. I looked at him and said, you do it.

So, if you're really interested in getting better and being the best of the best then you'll do whatever it takes to train every single day don't wait for your manager or your dealership to provide it go out there seek it and accomplish it that's what real winners do their self-motivated and self-starting people that's what you have to do those are the requirements to becoming successful if you want to be the best you will never achieve that unless you train every single day.

Professional Selling

What is professional selling? There is a lot that goes into it. You have many different facets, but one thing you always must remember is don't get mad at your money. Your customer is your money.

If you're communicating by text message or whatever means, the biggest thing to remember is don't be antagonistic on the phone or in a text message. Your first phone call is never going to be the best it's going to be a form of communication that you started with. Remember only 2% of any sale no matter what you're selling is sold on the first phone call, or the first contact.

Don't get discouraged. Remember you are going to communicate with this person at least 5 to 12 more times, so don't get frustrated because the calls not going the right way. Just remembered that your persistence is what's going to pull you through at the end of the day. Be agreeable, be respectful, and be able to understand what your customers looking for.

The key thing is to let them know that you're listening to what they're saying. Don't interrupt them, be professional. It's important that you acknowledge what they're saying, so they know that you are listening to them. Don't try to oversell whatever you're selling on that call, eventually you're going to get down to the meat and potatoes of that deal. But, it may take the seventh or the 10th phone call before that gets into the deal.

If you know the deal is going bad, the best thing to do is to tag the deal, flip the deal, get somebody else involved. Half of something is better than nothing, It maybe you just aren't the right fit for that customer or maybe the customer is not the right fit for you. But, tagging the deal or flipping the deal over to somebody else is right and the smart thing to do for all parties involved.

You can still be involved and hopefully make the deal turn into money. Then you can find out what went wrong get the feedback from the person you flip the deal to and find out what you could do differently. You can just sit there and listen to that other person talk to the customer. And turn a bad deal into a good deal. Move the conversation forward, and always be upbeat and thankful.

Building a rapport with the customer sometimes just isn't easy. But, if you can find some common ground and build off that, that usually would lead to closing a deal. When you're texting customer, sometimes what we're trying to say doesn't come across the way we originally meant. So, be clear about what you're saying in the text message. Be careful and think, about what you're going to say before you say it because you can't take it back.

PRODUCT KNOWLEDGE

For almost 30 years I have been talking about the subject and can't stress enough the importance of product knowledge. Every single manufacturer has some sort of online university that teaches about the product and its presentation. Ford Motor Company I think is one of the best platforms as far as teaching sales representative about product knowledge.

The worst thing that happens is when a customer walks in the door starts talking to a sales person about a vehicle that he wants, and that person knows more about the product than the salesperson does. I walked in to Best Buy and I was looking at televisions in the price range was $500 to almost $10,000. To me except for the size they all looked about the same there were some differences in color quality, but I really couldn't tell too much difference between what a $500 TV had to offer and a $5000 TV at the offer.

This young salesperson came up to me and said, "Sir, how may I help you?". So, we started up a small conversation and he right away recommended this TV that was $1800. And I said "Well thanks, but I really wanted to spend under $1000 on a new TV." Well he proceeded to tell me all the reasons why I wanted the $1800 TV versus the $500 TV.

He went through an in-depth product presentation on this TV that absolutely sold me, because of his professionalism, his product knowledge, and would seem to be his experience. I really couldn't find any good reason not to spend the extra money and buy the TV, which now I've had for almost 10 years and it still works perfectly.

It was because of a salesperson just like this that took the time out of his day to make me feel like I was the only customer in a store that happened to be packed at the time. He completely focused on me, my watching habits, my TV shows, the movies I liked, and showed me how to use everything on this TV.

At that point, I realized that the price just didn't matter. It didn't matter because money comes and goes every day, we work, we get paid, we spend, we work again, we get paid again, and we spend again. The difference is the stuff that we acquire stays with us and can stay with us for many years to come.

Just like that TV, I spent $1800 and I still have the TV which works perfect and looks great 10 years later. So now you got a family walks in the door at your dealership let's just say you're working at a Ford dealership and they're here to buy a new F150.

The F150 has multiple models you can get an XLT, a lariat, SXT, King Ranch, platinum, Limited. So now you must learn what the differences between all of these are. So, let's just say were talking about an XLT for example.

Now, you're with this family showing them an XLT and it happens to be what they want, you picked out the color, you picked out if it's a four-wheel-drive or 2 Will Drive. and now you're going over your features and benefits presentation.

I can tell you for sure is an old established rule that says if you spend 45 minutes talking about the most important things which are the features and benefits of the vehicle, you'll cut down your time to a minimum talking about the price and payment. This is something that cannot be truer.

So, now you sit there and you talk about the motor, and horsepower, and towing capacity, the warranty, and how the navigation systems work and how the backup camera works. spend all of your time teaching that customer all about the product knowledge that you have and how it everything works.

When you're done with your presentation whether it takes 30 minutes or two hours they are fully invested in the features and benefits of that vehicle they know how everything works how everything operates and everything they're getting.

By making sure that you are the absolute master of product knowledge, will build a serious amount of confidence between you and your customer and get the road to a sale underway to a delivery. The one thing that I always like to recommend is pick out of specific feature that intrigues you and make that your focal point because whatever that thing is that you personally like, you will learn everything about that particular feature and pass that knowledge off to your customer. this will give your customer great customer experience and that is what selling is about.

ATTITUDE

So, you woke up this morning had an argument with your significant other. On the way to work you got a speeding ticket. Then, you got to the dealership and spilled coffee on your pants and your shirt. After that, you went to get a pastry out of the vending machine and the machine took your dollar, you then found out when you left the dealership last night that your customer came in and bought, your deal went to another salesperson.

Your manager just chewed your butt because you were late this morning and missed the first five minutes of the sales meeting. Now, you go to your desk and there's brand-new salesperson sitting at your desk writing up a deal for customer.

I would say this is a bad start to any day wouldn't you. This is where your attitude comes in. Now you got two choices you can either go home be pissed off and say to heck with it all. Or you could walk to the bathroom look in the mirror splash a little water on your face and say to yourself, "Okay, I need an attitude adjustment. I'm not going to let this get to me, and then I'm going to turn this entire negative into a positive. I'm going to make my day pay."

This is the difference between a professional salesperson and somebody who's just not. To be able to clean yourself up brush yourself off and change your attitude takes a lot of work. You must suck it up get hold yourself shake it off and start over. Because your attitude will absolutely resonate, and your customers will absolutely see it all over your face. It will also cause you to not care because your disposition is negative since you woke up.

The discipline is no matter what leave all the negative at the front door and realize you are there to work to make money and to make the day pay not for you to pay for the day. Your attitude will make all the difference in the world on whether you make money or not. Don't let negative events affect your money. Always adjust your attitude and make sure no matter what you get a positive attitude to be you're disposition of the day.

Do you know how you can tell the difference between a true professional and one who is not? You can't tell what's going on in their personal life by looking at their face or their attitude. When you meet a professional, your meeting somebody with a smile on their face, dressed professional, and has a professional positive attitude ready and willing to give you the best customer service experience that you've ever had, that is a professional salesperson.

Made in the USA
Monee, IL
11 June 2022

97864704R00069